Berlitz®

Copenhagen

Front cover: The Little Mermaid statue
Right: Lur Players on Rådhuspladsen

Christiansborg. See the equestrian statue of Christian IX at the seat of the Danish Parliament. See page 39.

Amalienborg Slot. On duty at the home of the royal family. See page 56.

The Little Mermaid. The diminutive statue reclining on rocks in Langelinie. See page 59.

Vor Frelsers Kirke. Marvel at its spiralling staircase and copper-clad tower. See page 64.

Nyhavn. Copenhagen's colourful harbour, lined with bars and restaurants. See page 53.

Rosenborg Slot. The 17th-century palace houses the crown jewels. See page 51.

Nationalmuseet. Home of the famous Trundholm Sun Chariot. See page 45.

Roskilde. Visit Denmark's Viking heritage at this neat little town nearby. See page 80.

Ny Carlsberg Glyptotek. In a distinctive building is one of the world's foremost collections of classical art. See page 46.

Tivoli Gardens. The night-time illuminations are among its many attractions. See page 27.

A PERFECT DAY

9 am **Breakfast**

Indulge in a typically tasty breakfast: organic fruit and bread, soured milk sprinkled with brown sugar, pale Danish cheese and cold meat, and even a Danish pastry or two.

11.30am **Little Mermaid**

Tick her off your list by hopping aboard one of the 60-minute canal-boat tours, which depart from Nyhavn and sail all the way along the harbour. It's a true delight to see Copenhagen from the water, and this round trip will also give you a good awareness of where major sights are in the city.

10am **Hit the shops**

Stroll along pedestrianised Strøget, peeking into shop windows and making forays into the surrounding cobbled streets. Pop into Royal Copenhagen to admire Danish-designed home furnishings, silverware and porcelain, earmarking your favourites for later purchase.

11am **Coffee**

Cross Kongens Nytorv and head for the pretty painted wharf side at Nyhavn, one of the city's best people-watching places. Sit outside with a mid-morning coffee and watch the world go by.

12.30pm **Lunchtime**

Time to eat again! Wander along the harbour-side towards Frederiksholms canal, taking time to appreciate the Black Diamond and the buildings of Slotsholmen, before lunching on smørrebrød in the highly atmospheric Kanal Caféen (reservations are a must).

IN COPENHAGEN

5pm Dinner

Cross the harbour onto Christianshavn for a pre-dinner evening stroll around the always-interesting Christiania. You can eat at Spiseloppen, a delightfully cosy restaurant inside the Free Town; or treat yourself at one of Christianshavn's two Michelin-starred restaurants – Era Ora and the world-famous Noma (should you be lucky enough to get a table).

11pm On the town

At 11pm, Copenhagen's bright young things are just beginning to head out to the city's *hyggelig* bars and clubs. The Vesterbro district is good for nightlife – its lively Kødbyen area is the coolest place to laugh, drink and dance until the early hours.

2pm Culture fix

Spend a few hours exploring Danish history and culture, according to your interests. You're now very close to the fabulous Ny Carlsberg Glyptotek, Christiansborg and the National Museum; or a five-minute bus ride will take you to fairy-tale Rosenborg Slot, full of quirky details – look out for Queen Sophie Magdalene's lathe, Christian IV's spyhole, and a 17th-century joke chair that squirted its victims with water.

8pm Opera

The stunning new Opera House is on this side of the harbour – get your fix of Puccini or Bizet in a building so ultra-modern, you'll hardly know whether to look at the action on stage or the architecture.

CONTENTS

Introduction 9

A Brief History 13

Where to Go 25
❶ *Numbered map references pinpoint the sights*

Around Rådhuspladsen and Vesterbro . . . 25
City Hall 26, Lurs and Legends 27, Tivoli Gardens 27, Vesterbro 30

Strøget and Beyond 31
Strøget 32, Around Kongens Nytorv 34, South of Strøget 35, Gammelstrand 37

On and Around Slotsholmen 39
Christiansborg and its Museums 39, National Museum 45, Ny Carlsberg Glyptotek 46, Danish Design Centre 46

University Quarter and Parks 47
Copenhagen Cathedral 47, University and Gråbrødretorv 48, Round Tower 49, Postal Interlude 50, Rosenborg Slot 51, Fine Arts Museum 52

Nyhavn and Beyond 53
Amaliehavn Gardens 54, Amalienborg Palace 56, Churchill Park 58, The Little Mermaid 59, The Citadel 60, A Stroll Along Bredgade 61, Marble Church 62

Christianshavn And Holmen. 63

*Christians Kirke 64, Vor Frelsers Kirke 64,
Christiania 66, Opera House 66*

Outlying Districts 67

Frederiksberg 67, Nørrebro 68, Bispebjerg 69

Excursions. 69

*Store Magleby and Dragør 69, Open-Air Folk
Museum and Lyngby Lake 71, Arken 73, Louisiana
Museum of Modern Art 74, Helsingør 75,
Hillerød 78, Roskilde 80*

What to Do 85
Shopping 85
Entertainment. .90
Sports 93
Children's Copenhagen. 96

Eating Out 99

A–Z Travel Tips 117

Recommended Hotels 133

Index 140

Features

Bishop Absalon 15
Historical Landmarks 23
The Man Who Made Tivoli 32
Danish Thriller 42
Søren Kierkegaard 62
Across the Øresund to Malmö 81
Calendar of Events 98
Skål! ...and tak! 105

INTRODUCTION

Copenhagen (København), the capital of Denmark, is a charming seaside city with captivating architecture, history, culture, quirks and cuisine. Water is everywhere – the city is located on the eastern side of Zealand, the largest of Denmark's 400-plus islands, with only a narrow body of salt-sea, the Øresund (Strait), separating it from Sweden. About 1.7 million of the country's 5.6 million people call Copenhagen (and its surrounding metropolitan area) home. This compact little city heads a compact nation: Denmark itself is the smallest yet most densely populated nation in northern Europe, with over six times as many people per square kilometre as neighbouring Sweden.

Denmark is the only Scandinavian country physically connected to the European mainland – the Jutland peninsula is joined to northern Germany – and it forms both a literal and metaphorical bridge between Scandinavia and the rest of the continent. Denmark shares many of the characteristics of its Nordic neighbours: liberal welfare benefits coupled with a high standard of living, and a style of government that aims at consensus. Yet the country is also more 'European' than the rest of Scandinavia, and its appeal is universal.

Cosmopolitan Charm

In 1167, Bishop Absalon built a coastal castle at Havn, a strategic location at the mouth of the Baltic. Over the

Danish royalty

Denmark has the oldest royal dynasty in Europe, now headed by Queen Margrethe II – the nation's first reigning queen – and her French-born husband, Prince Henrik.

Equestrian statue of Frederik V at Amalienborg

centuries, a city grew up around it, and Copenhagen became the seat of royalty and the cultural and political centre that it is today. The green copper towers of churches, castles and cathedrals are scattered across the skyline – wander through cobbled streets and courtyards to discover the Christiansborg complex, Rosenborg Slot and the Amalienborg palaces, and a multitude of museums explaining their significance. Convivial Danes have made an art of the cosy coffee shop, and the city boasts some of the world's finest restaurants. Copenhagen is also renowned as one of northern Europe's jazz capitals – lively music and summer sunshine accompany shoppers as they stroll along Strøget, the longest pedestrianised street in the world. Its varied array of stores offer everything from handmade chocolates to cutting-edge clothing to Danish-designed homeware and furniture.

The People

Copenhagen's attractions are much wider than just history, culture and shopping; one of the city's great appeals is the character of the Danes themselves. The people are gregarious, loquacious and, at one and the same time, charming and sarcastic. They simply love enjoying life, especially when it comes to the combination of family, friends, food and, of course, copious amounts of alcohol. There is a word, *hygge*, almost untranslatable in English, that conveys a combination of warmth, wellbeing and intimacy that Danes incorporate into their lives as much as possible. A sense of *hygge* can be felt in

Strolling in Kongens Have

Canalside nightlife along Nyhavn

every part of Copenhagen, but is more obvious, especially on public holidays and warm sunny days, in the many parks, such as Rosenborg Have and Ørstedsparken, and popular meeting places like Rådhuspladsen and Nyhavn. Nowhere is it more evident than in that world-famous crown jewel of the city, Tivoli Gardens.

Fantasy and Culture

A strong sense of fantasy and colour fills the atmosphere in Copenhagen. Postmen wear bright red jackets and ride yellow bicycles, chimney sweeps pass by wearing black top hats and buses drive along with red-and-white Danish flags fluttering on both sides of the cab.

Although Copenhagen is a major capital city, it is very compact, with a well-preserved old-town area of winding cobbled streets, stuccoed houses and a network of canals, and almost everything is easily accessible by foot. Despite

Wooden boats are still being built at Roskilde using old skills

the fact that the reliable public transport system is superb, walking around Copenhagen is the best way to discover this city's inestimable charms.

Long before the phrase was immortalised in song by Danny Kaye, Copenhagen was known to be 'wonderful, wonderful' – a clean, green city full of gaiety, culture and charm, with a tradition of tolerance and humour.

Out and About

Within a very short distance of Copenhagen, and easily accessible on day trips, are three major places of interest: Roskilde, with its superb cathedral and Viking Ship Museum; Hillerød's beautiful Frederiksborg Castle; and Helsingør's Kronborg Castle, known to Shakespeare fans as Hamlet's home, Elsinore. Also worth a trip are Dragør, a picturesque fishing village near the airport; and the Louisiana Museum of Modern Art at Humlebæk, in a sublime setting on the coast just north of Copenhagen.

Sweden is just 4km (2.5 miles) away from Denmark at the narrowest point of the Øresund. The Swedish town of Helsingborg is a half-hour sail from Helsingør on one of the numerous ferries that ply the Sound. Malmö can be reached by road or rail over the Øresund Bridge in just 35 minutes.

A BRIEF HISTORY

Well before the Vikings organised themselves into an extraordinary nation of seafarers, Denmark was inhabited by hunting peoples. Prehistoric relics of all kinds – some dating back to 50,000BC – are displayed in Copenhagen's museums. The oldest surviving costumes in Europe have been found in this area, as have various musical instruments, including more than 30 examples of the Danish lur, which emits hoarse notes that seem strangely out of keeping with the long, graceful S-shaped stem characteristic of the instrument.

Viking Age

The first written records of the Vikings appear around AD800, at which time Viking raids on neighbouring European countries were becoming notorious. At their peak, these fearless warriors reached Newfoundland, rounded the North Cape, made sallies to Britain, Holland, France, Spain and the Mediterranean, and ended up as far afield as Russia, North Africa and the Middle East. Examples of their boats are on display at the Roskilde Viking Ship Museum (see page 83).

Danish raids upon England gathered in strength during the late 10th century and the first years of the 11th century, culminating in an attempt at conquest. Canute (Knud) the Great, after meeting considerable resistance, finally became King of England in 1016. The union was to last until 1042.

Christianity had been introduced into Denmark in 826 by a Benedictine monk, and received the royal seal of

Bymuseum

For a visual account of the city's colourful past and its better-known characters, call into Københavns Bymuseum (Vesterbrogade 59; tel: 33 21 07 72; www.bymuseum.dk; daily 10am–5pm; charge, Fri free).

The equestrian statue of Bishop Absalon on Højbro Plads

approval in 961 when King Harald (Bluetooth) was converted by a monk named Poppo. The monk is said to have convinced him by seizing red-hot irons in his bare hands. A large runic stone set up by Harald at Jelling in East Jutland records that he had 'won for himself all Denmark and Norway and made the Danes Christians.'

Medieval Times

In 1157, Valdemar I (the Great) came to the throne. He leaned heavily on the influence of Bishop Absalon of Roskilde, and this proved a partnership of critical importance to Copenhagen, then just a little fishing village called Havn. With its fine harbour on the Strait (Øresund in Danish) – the waterway between Denmark and Sweden, which forms the main entrance to the Baltic – the village found itself well-placed on what was becoming one of the main trading routes of medieval Europe.

War hero as well as statesman, Bishop Absalon fortified Havn by constructing a castle on its small harbour island of Slotsholmen in 1167; this is now acknowledged to be the founding date of the modern city. The name Havn became Køpmannæhafn ('merchants' harbour') in 1170, and eventually København. Today, Slotsholmen lies at the heart of the city. The impressive Christiansborg parliament buildings now occupy the site, but you can see some intriguing remnants of Absalon's castle in their cellars (see page 41).

In the 12th century Denmark sorely overextended itself in all directions, and for this it paid dearly in the 13th and 14th centuries. It had interfered in the government of Schleswig and Holstein as well as troubling the growing trade of the north German Hanseatic ports. The Germans marched into Jutland. The Danish aristocracy seized the opportunity to curb the powers of its monarchy, and in 1282 King Erik V was forced to sign a Great Charter under which he would rule together with the nobles in the Council of the Danish Realm.

Nevertheless, Valdemar IV Atterdag (c.1320–75), probably the greatest of medieval Danish kings, led the country back onto a path of conquests and into new conflict with its Nordic neighbours, setting a pattern that was to last, intermittently, for centuries. Denmark's hand was greatly strengthened

Bishop Absalon

Absalon (1128–1201), Bishop of Roskilde, Archbishop of Lund and founder of Copenhagen, was also a statesman, a crusader against the terrorising Wends, and a literary patron. His foster brother, Valdemar I, granted him the fishing village of Havn where Absalon built a stronghold on the site now occupied by Christiansborg (see page 39). The bishop commissioned his secretary, Saxo Grammaticus, to produce *Gesta Danorum*, an estimable history of Denmark.

Christian IV's Rosenborg Castle

when Valdemar's daughter Margrete married Håkon VI, King of Norway and Sweden. After his death, Margrete succeeded through the Treaty of Kalmar in 1397 in unifying the three Nordic powers under her great-nephew Erik VII of Pomerania. Indomitable Margrete ruled in his name, but was struck down by the plague at the peak of her power in 1412.

During the later, true reign of Erik VII (1412–39), Copenhagen was enlarged. The city then became the official Danish capital under Christopher III of Bavaria in the 1440s; when a university was founded by Christian I in 1479, it also became the country's cultural centre. By this time, the city's population had increased to about 10,000; Schleswig-Holstein was again under Danish rule; and a castle was being built at Helsingør (the Elsinore of Shakespeare's *Hamlet*) to enforce the payment of tolls on the Øresund. Control of the Øresund was vital to Denmark's strategic strength at the crossroads of the northern seas. Dues were exacted from each ship passing through the 4km (2.5-mile) wide channel between Helsingør on Zealand and Helsingborg in Sweden.

Denmark stood in a very strong position. However, the next 200 years proved to be a turbulent period, marked by civil war, the advent of Lutheranism, and Sweden's undying enmity following the infamous 1520 'Stockholm Bloodbath', when Danish King Christian II invited Stockholm's highest-ranking citizens to a banquet, then slaughtered 82 of them in the city square. This mass execution provoked the Swedish War of Liberation: the Kalmar Union collapsed as Sweden proclaimed its independence, although Denmark and Norway remained united.

The Reformation

In the 16th century, with the unprecedented spread of ideas, the latent, deep-seated discontent regarding abuses within the Catholic Church began to be brought out into the open. In Denmark, Catholic bishops had long been putting their wealth to political and military uses, and it was left to Christian III (1534–59) to break their stranglehold. In 1536 he declared himself supreme authority of a state church based on Lutheranism, which had made deep inroads since arriving from Germany. The bishops were imprisoned until they 'consented'.

Meanwhile, the wars with Sweden lurched disastrously on. By the latter half of the 17th century Denmark had been forced to relinquish her remaining Swedish possessions, and to cede the east bank of the Øresund to Sweden. This crucial waterway was now split down the middle, jointly controlled by the two Scandinavian powers, as it still is today.

As Denmark licked its many 17th-century war wounds, the city of Copenhagen had two great consolations. Firstly, the 60-year reign of larger-than-life Christian IV (1588–1648) saw a wave of new culture and fine architecture sweep the city. The 'Great Builder' doubled the size of Copenhagen, constructing many of the beautiful Renaissance buildings that make the city so uniquely photogenic today: the Round Tower, Børsen Stock Exchange, Rosenborg Castle. Then, in 1660, Copenhagen was declared a free city as an acknowledgement of its bravery during a two-year blockade by Sweden, meaning that all its residents were accorded the same privileges as the nobles.

Absolute Power

Christian IV's courage and vitality endeared him to his subjects, but involvement in the Thirty Years' War and continuing conflicts with Sweden were hugely damaging. By the time of Christian's death, Denmark was bankrupt and swathes of the country had been ceded. Political and social upheavals became inevitable.

In 1660, King Frederik III matched the mood of the moment and proclaimed himself absolute monarch, thereby depriving all the nobles of the Council of the Danish Realm of the powers they had enjoyed since 1282. Frederik's absolute rule presided over a period of national unity, with a tightly controlled, well-organised central bureaucracy.

The early absolutist kings still waged several costly wars, mainly against the Swedish. Copenhagen suffered a terrible plague in 1711–12 which killed 22,000 people – nearly a third of its inhabitants – as well as two devastating fires in 1728 and 1795.

The 18th century saw major social change. Serfdom was abolished in 1788 (note the Freedom Pillar in Vesterbrogade, opposite the Central Station) and peasants threw off the yoke of the medieval landlord and began to work for themselves. This emancipation gave the Danish countryside its present character of a landscape dotted with farms, and was of enormous influence in the shaping of modern Denmark.

Napoleon and the 19th Century

Denmark found itself reluctantly involved in the revolutionary wars of late-18th-century Europe. It attracted the wrath of the British by participating in the League of Armed Neutrality, an alliance with Russia, Sweden and Prussia that was intended to prevent Great Britain from searching neutral vessels at sea. In 1801, a fleet under admirals Nelson and Parker sailed into the bay of Copenhagen. During the ensuing battle, Nelson, so legend has it, raised a telescope to his blind eye so that he could deny having seen the signal to break off the engagement.

Afraid that Napoleon would take over the Dano-Norwegian fleet, Britain subsequently demanded its instant surrender. When the Danes refused to acquiesce, Copenhagen was blockaded and in 1807 subjected to a three-day bombardment by the British Navy. Denmark had no choice but to hand over what was left of its fleet to the British, only to be forced immediately afterwards to agree to an alliance with Napoleon, who was by then marching fast into Jutland.

When Napoleon was finally brought to his knees, Denmark emerged completely isolated on account of this alliance. Norway was handed over to Sweden in 1814 in payment of war debts and the formerly vast Danish territories overseas were reduced to Greenland, Iceland, the Faroes and the Virgin Islands. Fifty years later Denmark was further reduced by the loss of the duchies of Schleswig and Holstein – a third of its home territory and two-fifths of its population – to Bismarck's

Destruction of the Danish fleet during the Battle of Copenhagen

N.F.S. Grundtvig, priest, writer and pioneering educationalist

Prussia. Following a spate of civil turmoil in Denmark provoked by the 1848 revolution in France, Frederik VII was forced to relinquish his absolute rule and hand over the reins of power to the National Liberal Party.

A liberal constitution was drawn up with wide suffrage, and the Danish 'Golden Age' was all set to begin. In the city, Hans Christian Andersen (1805–75), the writer from Odense, strolled the streets, reading his fairy tales to groups of admirers. Factories and housing blocks for workers sprang up, so that by the late 19th century Copenhagen was a thriving industrial centre. Meanwhile, changes were beginning to take place in the countryside. The theologian and politician N.F.S. Grundtvig (1783–1872) established his system of popular adult high schools in 1844 to improve the peasant's lot.

The 20th Century

In 1901 an important landmark was reached in Danish constitutional history when a government based only on a majority in the lower chamber of parliament (Folketing) was appointed. The march of the common people brought them not only into the cities and urban areas, but also right into the political struggle. In 1915, the Liberal Democrats, Social

Democrats and Radical Liberals jointly forced the abolition of electoral privileges in the upper chamber and initiated a system of proportional representation for both chambers. At the same time, the vote was at last given to women and servants.

The new Danish society was put under severe strain as it struggled to maintain neutrality during World War I. After the war, north Schleswig voted itself back into Denmark, establishing the shape of today's border. Industrial unrest and economic depression between the two world wars failed to halt the progress of Denmark. In the design of consumer goods – furniture, cutlery, glass, pewter, silver and textiles – Denmark set new standards, combining utility with beauty, to the point where 'Danish design' became synonymous with good, functional, yet aesthetically pleasing articles.

When World War II broke out in 1939 the Scandinavian nations issued their declarations of neutrality. Nevertheless, on 9 April 1940 Denmark was invaded by Germany. After a token struggle, the country's defences collapsed and the nation fell under German control. However, the anti-Nazi sentiments of the vast majority of Danes were expressed by cold-shoulder treatment, and eventually acted upon through outright resistance. The Danes managed by various means to smuggle 7,000 of Denmark's 7,500 Jews out of the country and into neighbouring Sweden.

The wartime king, Christian X, elected to remain in Denmark during the Nazi occupation, becoming a symbol of independence and resistance. In 1943, his government resigned – it could no longer yield to German demands without losing the support of the population. The resistance was so organised that Denmark was already a full member of the Allied forces by the time the war came to an end in 1945. So began a new era of massive Danish reconstruction, resulting in the present modern-day society – one of the world's most successful attempts at a welfare state.

The Danish flag

Politically, Denmark abandoned neutrality when it became a member of NATO in 1949. Economically, it was a founding member of the European Free Trade Association (EFTA), and joined the European Economic Community (subsequently the European Union) with the UK and Ireland in 1972.

Modern Denmark

Denmark today is one of the most prosperous countries in Europe. At the World Summit in Copenhagen in 1995, Denmark was one of the only countries to forgive a sizeable amount of Third-World debt. However, increased immigration is challenging traditional ideas of Danish tolerance. In the 2001 elections the right-wing parties, on a platform of anti-immigration and law and order, formed a coalition government that endured for 10 years.

In September 2005, Danish foreign affairs took a turn for the worse when a national newspaper published 12 cartoons of the Prophet Muhammad, causing protests and boycotts, particularly in the Muslim world.

Although Denmark's population of around 5.6 million enjoys an extremely high standard of living, the aftermath of the 2008 financial crisis is putting pressure on the generous provisions of the welfare state. Denmark's first female prime minister, Helle Thorning-Schmidt, was elected in late 2011 and immediately faced tough political challenges, including Denmark's fraught six months holding the EU Presidency in 2012 and an unpopular austerity budget in 2013.

Historical Landmarks

1167 King Valdemar the Great gives Bishop Absalon land by the Øresund; Absalon fortifies the fishing and trading settlement of Havn.

1254 The village of Køpmannæhafn receives a municipal charter. The Hanseatic League uses the port as a staging post for Baltic trade.

1376 Absalon's castle is replaced by København Slot.

1397–1534 Denmark sets up the Kalmar Union with Norway and Sweden.

1417 Erik VII makes Copenhagen his capital. Ships on the Øresund have to pay tolls from 1425. Trade flourishes; the population rises to 10,000.

1479 The university is founded by Christian I.

1588–1648 Christian IV enlarges the town and harbour and commissions grand Renaissance-style buildings, including Rosenborg Slot and Børsen. The Thirty Years' War destroys Denmark's prosperity.

1660 Copenhagen is declared a free city.

1711–12 Plague kills nearly one third of Copenhagen's inhabitants.

Early 1800s The British fleet under Nelson demands the surrender of the Danish fleet in the Napoleonic Wars. Bombardment ruins the city.

Late 1800s Denmark's 'Golden Age' of arts and science. The first railway line links Copenhagen with Roskilde; city ramparts are demolished; industrialisation draws in country people.

1914–18 Denmark remains neutral during World War I.

1918 Christiansborg Palace becomes the seat of the Danish parliament.

1924 Social Democrats win power; a welfare state is established.

1940–5 Denmark is occupied by German forces.

1950–70 Modern satellite towns spring up around Copenhagen.

1971 Young people establish the Free State of Christiania.

1972 Margrethe II is crowned. Denmark joins the EEC.

2000 Øresund Bridge opens between Denmark and Sweden.

2001 Election of right-wing government; policy to restrict immigration.

2005–6 'Muhammad drawings' in the *Jyllands-Posten* newspaper push the government into a major diplomatic crisis.

2012 Queen Margrethe's 40th jubilee. A previously unknown Hans Christian Andersen story, *The Tallow Candle*, is discovered.

WHERE TO GO

You will have no problem finding your way around this delightfully compact city. Most of the important sights and museums are contained within the central section and bounded by the former medieval ramparts, so exploring Copenhagen on foot is a real pleasure. The network of canals also offers many opportunities for waterside walks and gentle excursions afloat. And if you want a change of pace from sightseeing or shopping, the abundance of leafy parks and attractive gardens provides a very welcome and pleasant retreat.

AROUND RÅDHUSPLADSEN AND VESTERBRO

Every city has a social gathering point, but Copenhagen has more than one. Without a doubt, the centrally located **Rådhuspladsen** (City Hall Square) is the most popular and, consequently, most of the suggested planned walks start from here. It is also the stopping point for the main bus routes and is near Central Station, where trains depart for the suburbs and beyond.

It is in this large open square, with its buskers and ubiquitous hot-dog stands *(pølsevogn)*, that you can take the opportunity to observe Danish life.

> **Museum entry**
>
> Museum opening times and charges are subject to change. It is advisable to check the listings in the free guide, *Copenhagen This Week*. The Copenhagen Card (see page 130) offers free or discounted entry.

Hans Christian Andersen, author and poet

Rådhuspladsen, focal point of city life

City Hall

The dominant building in Rådhuspladsen is the red-brick **Rådhus** ❶ (City Hall; Mon–Fri 8am–5pm, Sat 9.30am–1pm; free), with its 105m (345ft) tower. Built between 1892 and 1905, it is reached via broad steps which play host to impromptu concerts. Its main doorway is crowned by a statue of Bishop Absalon, the founder of the city, in copper and 22-carat gilt. On the roof above you'll see six bronze figures of night watchmen dating from various periods of the city's history. Each section of the Rådhus bears a different style and imprint, but they come together architecturally very much like a patchwork quilt. The main hall and banqueting room are impressive with their statuary and coats-of-arms – especially the view of the 44m (145ft) long hall from the first-floor colonnade (guided tours in English Mon–Fri 3pm, Sat 10am; tel: 33 66 25 82; www.kk.dk; charge).

If you are feeling energetic, there are also guided tours of **City Hall Tower** and its 300 steps (Mon–Fri 11am and 2pm, Sat noon; charge). On a clear day you can see north along the coast and across the Øresund to Sweden. In the foyer of City Hall a sign points to **Jens Olsen's World Clock** (Mon–Fri 8.30am–4.30pm, Sat 10am–1pm; charge). This intriguing astronomical clock, said to have more than 14,000 parts, shows time around the world, the positions of the planets and the Gregorian calendar.

Lurs and Legends

To your right as you leave the City Hall, on Vester Voldgade, is the unique **Lur Players** statue. Legend has it that the two men on top will sound a note on their instruments if a virgin passes by – they've been standing on the column since 1914 but have led a life of silence. On the opposite corner of the square is the dramatic copper **Bull-and-Dragon Fountain** (1923), depicting a fierce, watery battle between the two beasts. Not far away sits a bronze version of Denmark's favourite son, storyteller Hans Christian Andersen, near the boulevard that bears his name. It is on this busy road that you'll notice a very prominent feature of Danish life – the ubiquitous bicycle.

Lur Players on Rådhuspladsen

The road to the northwest of Rådhuspladsen is Vesterbrogade, which leads to Central Station, the **Copenhagen Visitor Centre** (see page 130) and Tivoli Gardens.

Tivoli Gardens

Across Hans Christian Andersens Boulevard from

Night-time illuminations at Tivoli's pagoda

Rådhuspladsen is Copenhagen's most famous attraction, **Tivoli Gardens** ❷ (main entrance Vesterbrogade 3; tel: 33 15 10 01; www.tivoli.dk; daily mid-Apr to mid-Sept Sun–Thur 11am–10pm, Fri 11am–12.30am, Sat 11am–midnight; also open Halloween and Christmas – see website for hours; charge).

Opened in 1843, this old-time pleasure park offers a joyous combination of theatrical performances, concerts, cafés and restaurants, and funfair rides and amusements, all set in beautiful gardens in the heart of the city. Visitors are welcomed by attendants dressed in old-fashioned outfits who embody a sense of dignity and tradition – qualities that infuse Tivoli. At the Pantomime Theatre, for instance, the mimed antics of Harlequin, Columbine and the clown Pierrot are accompanied not by pre-recorded music but by a small orchestra. The Tivoli Boys' Guard brass band frequently parades through the park, dressed in red-and-white uniforms and bearskin caps.

Another 19th-century tradition is the fireworks display that begins and ends the opening season.

Rollercoaster Rides & Amusements

With its lake and lawns, water features and prolific flower-beds, Tivoli fulfils its role as a traditional landscaped garden. Archaic side stalls, a traditional merry-go-round and a vintage trolleybus ride add to the feeling that you have stepped back into an older, gentler era. But it's not all coconut shies and hoopla – there are plenty of modern rides to set the pulse racing. Himmelskibet is the tallest carousel in the world, twirling its riders along at a height of 80m (262ft). The most extreme of the park's four rollercoasters is Dæmonen, which loops-the-loop at speeds of up to 80kph (50mph). Vertigo, one of the newest rides, simulates a flight in a fighter jet.

For kids, excitements include a Viking-ship roundabout, flying aeroplanes and miniature classic cars. For the even fainter of heart, the dragon boats on the lake have a romantic appeal. To go on any of the rides you need to either buy a multi-ride pass (199kr), which lasts all day, or separate tickets (25kr–75kr).

Night-time Wonderland

As darkness falls, the atmosphere changes as thousands of multicoloured lights illuminate the park and its fairy-tale buildings, and music fills the air. The open-air stage is the focus for spectacular productions, such as *A Tivoli Fairy-tale* celebrating Hans Christian Andersen. On Friday evenings the Glassalen is the venue for pop and rock concerts featuring bands from Denmark and abroad. Jazz, blues and swing are all on the Tivoli programme. For

Christmas at Tivoli

Tivoli throws open its doors for the festive season in the run-up to Christmas each year. The lake is frozen for skating and stalls offer tempting seasonal wares.

Thrilling rides are all part of the fun at Tivoli

classical music, check out the main Concert Hall, home of the Copenhagen Philharmonic (http://copenhagenphil.dk). Many of the performances are free.

Tivoli's 40 bars and restaurants are favourite meeting places for friends, families and business people, and range from cafés to top-quality restaurants. It can be difficult to get a seat on warm summer evenings, so book ahead.

Vesterbro

Turn left out of the main Tivoli gate onto Vesterbrogade. The **Freedom Pillar** monument commemorates the end of serfdom in Denmark in 1788, and marks the start of Vesterbro, once a down-at-heel district known for its slaughterhouses and red-light area. Today it's on the up, with quirky boutiques and snug cafés. Some of the city's trendiest clubs and restaurants have moved into the former meat-packing sector **Kødbyen** ❸, making it one of the best places in town for evening entertainment – turn left down Colbjørnsensgade, then right onto Halmtorvet to find it.

No visit to Copenhagen is complete without sampling the local brew at **Carlsberg Brewery** (Gammel Carlsbergvej 11, Valby; www.visitcarlsberg.com; Tue–Sun 10am–5pm; charge), right on the edge of Vesterbro – either meander through the district, or hop on bus 18 or 26. The brewery's founder, Jacob Christian Jacobsen (1811–87), wanted to prove that industrial enterprises could be beautiful as well as functional, and so the whole site is surprisingly ornate. Gargoyles and lotus flowers decorate the Carlsberg chimney, while the Renaissance-style brew house is adorned with mosaics and sculptures. Jacob named his beer Carlsberg after his son, Carl (1842–1914). But father and son did not see eye to eye and Carl eventually opened his own brewery next door. You can find out more about the family – and the beer – at the Visitors' Centre.

STRØGET AND BEYOND

One of the first places you'll visit after Rådhuspladsen is Copenhagen's most famous pedestrian-only street. Known as **Strøget ④** (pronounced stroy-et), this is a continuation of four streets – Frederiksberggade (leading off Rådhuspladsen), Nygade Vimmelskaftet, Amagertorv and Østergade – that wind their way for 1km (0.6 miles) to Kongens Nytorv (King's New Square). This traffic-free haven offers visitors an amazing assortment of shops, along with numerous small

Strøget musician

bars, restaurants, cafés and an abundance of street performers. Wander off Strøget to explore the small side streets: each of these has its own surprises among the numerous antiques shops, speciality stores, boutiques and fashionable restaurants.

Strøget

The entrance to Frederiksberggade, dominated by fast-food outlets, is not exactly prepossessing; however, perseverance will bring its rewards. Where Frederiksberggade ends, Strøget opens out into two squares on either side of the street. **Gammeltorv**, to the left, is a popular place for small market stalls and is home to the **Caritas Fountain** which, dating from 1610, is the city's oldest. In a tradition going back to the golden wedding of King Christian IX and Queen Louise in 1892, imitation golden apples are made to dance on the jets of the fountain on the monarch's birthday (now 16 April). **Nytorv**, to the right, is dominated by the impressive architecture of the law courts. Each of these squares is a

The Man Who Made Tivoli

The driving force behind Tivoli was the 19th-century polyglot entrepreneur Georg Cartensen. He had travelled widely and seen the idea in practice in cities such as Paris. His vision was to combine a pleasure garden with venues for cultural events and a fair. But first he had to persuade the king, Christian VIII, of his plan's viability. The king gave his assent 'to provide the masses with suitable entertainment and fun', and Tivoli opened its doors to the public in August 1843. Crowds flocked to the gardens to see pantomimes, shows and fireworks displays and enjoy the rides, fairground stalls and concerts. Among the first attractions was a cable-car ride. Over the years, Tivoli has been modernised and extended, but its magic is undiminished and it still retains a special place in the hearts of the Danes.

Royal Copenhagen Porcelain

good place to sit at a street café and watch the procession of passing people.

The next place of note is the **Helligåndskirken** (Church of the Holy Spirit). Built in the 17th–18th century, it is set in its own small gardens. Outside is an area particularly popular with street performers and other hawkers. Just past this point, Strøget opens out again and on the left side of Amagertorv you'll see a fine example of Dutch baroque buildings – home to the group of **Royal Copenhagen** shops (see page 87). One of these, at No. 6, is the Royal Copenhagen Porcelain store, an Aladdin's cave with an elegant restaurant. It dates from 1616. Next door, Georg Jensen features tableware sets designed over the last century. For the best of Danish design, pop in to Illums Bolighus at No. 10, an elegant department store featuring kitchenware, lighting and furniture.

As Amagertorv becomes Østergade, the shops become even more upmarket. Pause to look in the window of Halberstadt

Kongens Nytorv, with the statue of Christian V

(No. 4) – a jeweller founded in 1846 – which features a small golden train encrusted with diamonds and gems that runs continually around.

Around Kongens Nytorv

Kongens Nytorv ❺, the 'King's New Square' of Christian V – dating from 1680 and still the city's largest (12 streets lead off it) – is surrounded by impressive stately buildings. The park in the centre of the square is dominated by the king himself, in the form of an elaborate equestrian statue, with four classical figures seated submissively under his horse.

On the southwest side is the Old Stage of **Det Kongelige Teater** (Danish Royal Theatre; www.kglteater.dk). It was founded in 1748, and was briefly the stage of Hans Christian Andersen at the age of 14, who tried without success to become a ballet dancer. This venerable old building, the spiritual home of Denmark's national ballet, opera and theatre, has now relinquished many of its performances to two new state-of-the-art buildings: the Royal Danish Playhouse (Skuespilhuset) at Skt Annæ Plads; and, facing it across the water, the Opera House (Operan; see page 66).

Next to the theatre stands **Charlottenborg Slot**, the oldest building on the square. It was built as a royal palace in 1683 in the style of Dutch baroque and, since 1754, has been the home of the Royal Danish Academy of Fine Arts. Enter through the front gate and at the rear is **Kunsthal Charlottenborg**, which exhibits Danish and international contemporary art (www. kunsthalcharlottenborg.dk; Tue–Sun 11am–5pm, to 8pm Wed; charge).

Look around the square and you will notice other splendid buildings. **Thotts Palae** (Thott's Mansion), in the northeast corner, was built for the naval hero Admiral Niels Juel and is now home to the French Embassy. Not to be outdone is the wonderful facade of the **Hotel D'Angleterre**, one of Denmark's finest hotels.

The unusually shaped building on the corner of Nyhavn (see page 53), tucked between Store Strandstræde and Bredgade, is the beautifully preserved 1782 **Kanneworffs Hus**, which houses the jewellery shop House of Amber and a small **Amber Museum** (www.houseofamber.com; May–Sept daily 10am–6.30pm, Oct–Apr daily 10am–5.30pm; charge). Diagonally across the square is the imposing seven-storey **Magasin du Nord**, with its impressive ornate facade. This was Scandinavia's first department store and is still its largest.

South of Strøget

Leave Kongens Nytorv by Vingårdsstræde at the southwest corner of Magasin du Nord. You'll find yourself in an area of jazz clubs, small bars and artists' hang-outs. At its junction with Admiralgade is the massive 70m (230ft) tall copper spire

Holmens Kirke, the sailors' church

of **Skt Nicolai Kirke** (St Nicholas Church). Destroyed several times by fire and rebuilt as recently as 1917, it houses the Copenhagen Contemporary Art Centre, **Nikolaj Kunsthal** (www.nikolajkunsthal.dk; Tue–Sun noon–5pm, Thur until 9pm; charge, Wed free), which has a small permanent collection and an innovative programme of temporary exhibitions. At the south end of Admiralgade is **Holmens Kirke** (Mon–Fri 10am–3pm, until 4pm in summer, Sat 9am–noon; free). The church is in the Venetian style, but with Dutch gable ends and a small copper tower in the middle. The building was originally a 16th-century anchor forge, but was transformed in 1619 by Christian IV into a sailors' church. On the altar, reredos and pulpit there is a profusion of oak carvings by Abel Schrøder the Younger. Look for the model ship hanging from the ceiling, a tradition common in many Danish churches. There are also free organ concerts on Wednesdays at noon (July and August).

Outside Holmens Kirke you are now by the canal, and it is impossible not to be impressed by the Christiansborg complex on the opposite bank (see page 39). Turn right up Ved Stranden and head for the Højbro bridge and the junction with Gammelstrand and Højbro Plads.

Within a short distance of here are three very different statues. The most obvious of these, on **Højbro Plads**, is the magnificent copper green **equestrian statue of Bishop Absalon** showing the warrior-priest in chain mail with axe in hand. On the corner of Gammelstrand stands the **statue of the Fiskerkone** (Fisherman's Wife), scarf on her head, shawl around her shoulders, wearing an apron and clasping a fish. Erected in 1940, she resembles the women who for centuries sold fish along the wharf. The third sculpture is less obvious; in fact, you'll have to look over the bridge to discover the submerged legend of the **'Merman with Seven Sons'**, who appeal to their human mother Agnete to return to them. It is attractively illuminated at night.

Gammelstrand

Next, turn into Gammelstrand itself; the name means 'old shore' and, as this implies, it is the former edge of the city. This is one of the two principal starting points for canal-boat tours, the other being in Nyhavn (see page 53). Immediately across the canal lies a distinctive square-arched, yellow-ochre building with a classical-style frieze, looking like a national tomb: a monument to the great Danish sculptor Bertel Thorvaldsen (1770–1844; see page 42). Off to the right, on Frederiksholms Kanal, you'll be able to make out the arched entrance to the

A royal favourite

Holmens Kirke remains a favourite with the royal family. In 1967 Queen Margrethe was married here to Prince Henrik, formerly the French Count de Laborde de Montpezat.

Vandkunsten square

colossal Nationalmuseet (see page 45). Gammelstrand also has restaurants and bars, among which is the elegant **Krogs** seafood restaurant.

Time now to proceed back to Rådhuspladsen, via a collection of interesting old streets. At the western end of Gammelstrand, Snaregade features some timber-framed houses. Continue into Magstræde, where the houses at numbers 17 and 19 are two of the city's oldest, dating from 1640. Next is **Vandkunsten**, a delightful little square with outdoor cafés and a pretty fountain. The name of the square means 'water artifice' and it is here that Copenhagen's first water pipes were laid. Continue across the next junction into Gåsegade, and look for the gabled houses with 18th-century hoists at the top. Furniture is traditionally hauled up by these hoists, rather than being squeezed up the narrow stairwells.

On the corner of Hestemøllestræde and Lavendelstræde is a house where Mozart's widow lived with her second husband, a Danish diplomat. Here, the huge archways of Copenhagen's fourth town hall dominate; built between 1805 and 1815, it now houses the law courts. On Lavendelstræde you'll find typical Danish houses and shops from 1796, the year after the city's second great fire, and at the end of the street Vester Voldgade leads to Rådhuspladsen.

ON AND AROUND SLOTSHOLMEN

Starting at Rådhuspladsen, retrace your steps on the previous tour back to the Højbro bridge and then cross it to the small island of Slotsholmen (Castle Island) and the imposing towers of Christiansborg. Stop a little further along the canal at the highly ornamented **Børsen** ❻ (Stock Exchange), dating from the days of Christian IV. Its green copper roof is topped by a spire composed of four entwined dragons' tails. Christian IV was influenced by the booming Netherlands architecture of his day, and in 1619 commissioned two Dutch brothers to design the building. Currently it houses special events, and the Stock Exchange has since emigrated to Strøget.

Christiansborg and its Museums

Christiansborg ❼ is the fifth castle or palace to have stood on this site since Absalon built his fortress in 1167: pillage, fire and rebuilding frenzies have taken their toll on the earlier ones. The second castle became the permanent seat of the king and government in 1417. The present edifice dates from the early 20th century, at which time Thorvald Jørgensen won an architectural competition for the design of a new Christiansborg palace. On 15 November 1907, King Frederik VIII laid the cornerstone that had been hewn out of the granite remains from Absalon's original castle. Above this a vast plinth was made of 7,500 boulders donated by 750 Danish boroughs, and then the palace was faced with granite slabs. Look up to see 57 granite

Harbour bus

Give your feet a rest with a trip on the harbour bus, which connects the Royal Library's Black Diamond building with the Little Mermaid, stopping at Holmen, Nyhavn and the Opera House en route.

masks of Denmark's greatest men. Covered in copper between 1937 and 1939, the roof of Christiansborg makes an imposing addition to the city's verdigris skyline.

The chapel, theatre museum, riding stables and beautifully restored **Marmorbroen** (Marble Bridge), which survived two disastrous fires in 1794 and 1884, help to give the palace a more venerable aspect than its more recent origins suggest. Today the castle (nicknamed 'Borgen', as in the name of the award-winning Danish political TV series) houses government ministries, Parliament (Folketing) and the Danish Supreme Court, as well as being the centre of a complex of museums.

The most notable highlights of the complex include the **Kongelige Repræsentationslokaler** (Royal Reception Chambers; tel: 33 92 64 92; www.ses.dk; May–Sept daily 10am–5pm, Oct–Apr Tue–Sun 10am–5pm; guided tours in

Christiansborg, seat of the Danish Parliament

English daily 3pm; charge). One of the guide's first anecdotes will probably be: 'Look at the roof here, held by pillars in the shape of male statues, heads bent to take the weight – a symbol of modern Danes paying their taxes…' You can also visit the Reception Rooms on your own.

Marble Bridge, built in 1745

The chambers, on the first floor, are used by the Queen and Prime Minister for official receptions, state banquets, and royal audiences with foreign ambassadors. They are richly decorated with works of art retrieved from the earlier palaces, as well as pieces by modern Danish artists. Most impressive is the 40m (130ft) long Great Hall hung with a series of tapestries by Bjørn Nørgaard recounting the history of Denmark. They were a 50th birthday present for Queen Margrethe II. Made by Les Gobelins in Paris, they took 10 years to complete. Other chambers include the Throne Room and the balcony overlooking Slotspladsen (Castle Square), from where monarchs are proclaimed.

In the palace basement you will find the extensive **Ruinerne af Absalons Borg** (Ruins of Absalon's Palace; May–Sept daily 10am–5pm; Oct–Apr Tue–Sun 10am–5pm; charge) from 1167, as well as remnants of more recent castles on the site. Also in the complex is the **Folketing** (Danish Parliament; tel: 33 37 32 21; www.ft.dk; guided tours in English 1pm Sun year round, also Mon–Fri 1pm July to mid-Aug; free).

Out in the vast parade ground, dominated by a copper equestrian statue of Christian IX, are the **Kongelige Stalde og Kareter** (Royal Stables; May–Sept daily 1.30–4pm,

Oct–Apr Tue–Sun 1.30–4pm; charge). The stables are home to some fine driving and riding horses, which can sometimes be seen exercising in the square. On display are uniforms and royal state carriages dating from 1778.

Theatre Museum

In an elegant terrace above the stables is the **Teatermuseet** (Theatre Museum; www.teatermuseet.dk; Tue–Thur 11am–3pm, Sat–Sun 1–4pm; charge). The delightful little auditorium and galleries are packed with costumes, set models and other theatrical relics.

Thorvaldsens Museum

Throngs of painted people decorate the ochre facade of **Thorvaldsens Museum ⑧** (www.thorvaldsensmuseum.dk; Tue–Sun 10am–5pm; charge, Wed free), on the Gammelstrand side of Christiansborg. The museum is dedicated to the

Danish Thriller

Across Scandinavia, Nordic Noir has hit the big time. Although Denmark hasn't (yet) produced a popular crime writer with the stature of a Henning Mankell, Stieg Larsson or Jo Nesbø, it has made a huge impact in TV terms. From the moment detective Sarah Lund stepped into the frame in The Killing (Forbrydelsen; 2007), viewers were hooked. The equally addictive Borgen (2010) followed, about a politician, Birgitte Nyborg, who becomes the first female prime minister of Denmark. Finally came The Bridge (Broen; 2011), which begins in suitably grisly fashion with the discovery of a bisected corpse on the Øresund Bridge, half lying in Denmark and half in Sweden... The final series of The Killing was screened in Britain in 2013: those suffering withdrawal symptoms can take a location tour with **Peter and Ping** (tel: 27 12 89 51; www.peter-og-ping.dk; 4pm Sat from Vesterport Station; charge).

A royal carriage on display in Christiansborg's stables

celebrated Danish sculptor Bertel Thorvaldsen (1770–1844) who, at the tender age of 11, was accepted into the Copenhagen Art Academy. Later he won a scholarship to Rome, where he lived and worked for more than 40 years. On his triumphant return to Denmark, he chose a young architect, Gottlieb Bindesbøll, to design a museum to house his sculptures. The result is one of Copenhagen's most distinctive buildings, both inside and out, its richly coloured walls contrasting with the pure white plaster and marble of Thorvaldsen's sculptures.

Arsenal Museum

In a side street behind the Royal Stables, **Tøjhusmuseet** (Arsenal Museum, Tøjhusgade 3; www.thm.dk; Tue–Sun noon–4pm; charge) holds a fascinating collection of military items, including an early 15th-century cannon from the time of Queen Margrete I and sophisticated modern weapons. Attendants wearing three-cornered hats and knee-length red

The tranquil gardens of the Royal Library

jackets greet you as you enter the vast 400-year-old building. Cannonballs are piled high like potatoes and old military planes are suspended from the roof. The Armoury Hall on the first floor was completely revamped in 2012/2013 and now houses a permanent exhibition about Denmark's bellicose past.

Royal Library

Close by are the **Royal Library Gardens** (daily 6am–10pm). Designed in 1920, the gardens are a veritable oasis of peace and calm, and an ideal place to sit and rest. Although the building you see from the gardens only dates from 1906, Frederik III founded **Det Kongelige Bibliotek** (Royal Library; www. kb.dk) around 1653. Later it was merged with the University Library, founded in 1482. Walk around the building to the waterfront and be prepared for a huge architectural surprise. On Søren Kierkegaards Plads a seven-storey, glass, granite, concrete and steel structure appears to be leaning towards the river. This, because of its colour, is affectionately known as **Den Sorte Diamant** (The Black Diamond), and is the annexe for the Royal Library. Concerts, lectures and meetings are also held here, and there are excellent shops, restaurants and cafés.

An architectural masterpiece on a very different scale is Daniel Libeskind's conversion of the Royal Boat House into the **Dansk Jødisk Museum** (Danish Jewish Museum; Proviantpassagen 6; www.jewmus.dk; June–Aug Tue–Sun 10am–5pm, Sept–May Tue–Fri 1–4pm, Sat–Sun noon–5pm; charge). This unexpected find in the Royal Library Gardens tells the story of Denmark's Jews, their cultural heritage and daily life, through its collection of paintings, photographs, artefacts, memoirs, films and audio recordings.

National Museum

Leaving Slotsholmen by the Marble Bridge, turn right and follow the canal to Ny Vestergade and the **Nationalmuseet** ❾ (National Museum; www.natmus.dk; Tue–Sun 10am–5pm; free). The biggest museum in Scandinavia, it focuses on Danish history from the Stone Age to modern times. One of the most striking exhibits is the Trundholm Sun Chariot (1200BC), dating from a period when the Danes worshipped the sun, imagining it as a disc of gold riding through the sky in a chariot behind a celestial horse. Other sections of the museum contain ethnographic exhibits from

Cannon in the Arsenal Museum

around the world (including a reconstructed Inuit camp from Greenland), classical antiquities and the Royal Coin and Medal Collection. A hands-on Children's Museum provides an interesting diversion for youngsters.

Ny Carlsberg Glyptotek

From the Nationalmuseet, cross over Hans Christian Andersens Boulevard and head for the distinctive classical building with a columned portal and domed roof, which houses **Ny Carlsberg Glyptotek** ❿ (Dantes Plads 7; www.glyptoteket.dk; Tue–Sun 11am–5pm; charge, Sun free). The Glyptotek was founded on the classical collection of Carl Jacobsen (1842–1914), a Danish brewer and art connoisseur. Under its elaborate roof lies one of the world's foremost displays of Egyptian, Greek, Roman and Etruscan art. A sub-tropical garden in the central hall appears to have been transplanted directly from ancient Rome. In contrast, the French collection – works by Gauguin, van Gogh and Monet, Rodin sculptures and a complete set of Degas bronzes – is in a glorious modern wing, built in 1996 and designed by Henning Larsen (creator of Copenhagen's Opera House).

A good deed

The word *mitzvah* on the door of the Danish Jewish Museum means 'a good deed'. It relates to the remarkable rescue in 1943 of 7,000 Jews who, in the face of deportation to Nazi concentration camps, were hidden and taken in small boats to Sweden.

Danish Design Centre

Denmark is justly renowned for its modern design classics, celebrated across the road at the **Dansk Design Center** ⓫ (Hans Christian Andersens Boulevard 27; www.ddc.dk; check website for opening times), which underwent a complete redesign in 2013.

Ny Carlsberg Glyptotek's domed roof and sub-tropical garden

UNIVERSITY QUARTER AND PARKS

From Rådhuspladsen, go northwest for a short way along Vester Voldgade and then turn right into narrow Studiestræde, home to a melange of antiques shops, bookstalls and boutiques gathered in an 18th-century setting.

At Studiestræde 6 a plaque records that H.C. Ørsted, who discovered electro-magnetism in 1820, lived here. A few metres further on, at the corner of Nørregade, is one of Copenhagen's oldest preserved buildings, the former Bispegården (Bishop's Residence), built in 1500 and part of the university. Nearby on Bispetorvet, a 1943 monument commemorates the 400th anniversary of the introduction of the Reformation to Denmark.

Copenhagen Cathedral

At the end of Studiestræde stands the **Domkirke** 12 (Cathedral)

Picturesque Gråbrødretor

of Copenhagen, known as **Vor Frue Kirke** (Church of Our Lady; www.koebenhavnsdomkirke.dk; daily 8am–5pm; free). Bishop Absalon's successor, Sunesen, is said to have laid its foundations in the 12th century, but by 1316 it had already burned down four times. Later, two further constructions were destroyed – by the great 1728 fire and by British bombardment in 1807. The present church was reconstructed by V.F.K. and C.F. Hansen between 1811 and 1829. Its austere interior is relieved by a collection of heroic statues by Bertel Thorvaldsen: 12 massive marble Apostles line the aisle, while an orange-lit altar is surrounded by bronze candelabra and dominated by his figure of Christ.

University and Gråbrødretorv

Proceed along the north side of the Cathedral. On the left is the main Copenhagen University block, which dates back in its present form only as far as the 1830s. The university was founded in 1479. This is a typical student area with a number of interesting bookshops and cafés.

Turn right into Fiolstræde, a lively spot for alfresco dining, and left into Skindergade, which leads into **Gråbrødretorv** (Greyfriar's Square), a large, picturesque traffic-free square surrounded by brightly painted 18th-century houses. It was the site of a Franciscan monastery until the Reformation. Cafés and restaurants proliferate here.

Round Tower

Continue along Skindergade to Købmagergade and you'll find yourself at the foot of one of Copenhagen's most beloved landmarks, the **Rundetaarn** ⑬ (Round Tower; www.rundetaarn.dk; daily mid-May to mid-Sept 10am–8pm, mid-Sept to mid-May 10am–5pm; charge). The Round Tower was built by Christian IV in 1642 as part of his vision to provide an astronomical observatory, church and university library for 17th-century scholars. You can walk to the top of the 36m (118ft) high tower, but not by any ordinary means – steps would have been impractical for raising the heavy equipment needed here. Instead, a wide spiral ramp, 210m (690ft) long, winds around inside the tower. Not only did Tsar Peter the Great ride up to the top on horseback in 1716, but his empress followed him in a horse-drawn coach. There is a splendid view over the rooftops of the old city from the top. **Trinitatis Kirke** (Trinity Church) is to the rear of the tower; look through the glass panel in the wall at the bottom of the ramp. The library hall above is now used for exhibitions and concerts.

Old observatory

The Rundetaarn (Round Tower) has the oldest functioning observatory in Europe. If you happen to be here in winter, you can view the night sky through its telescope (late Nov–Mar Tue–Wed 7–10pm).

The building across Købmagergade from the Round Tower, at the corner with Krystalgade, is the Regensen university hostel. Although students have lived here since 1623, most of the present structure dates from the 18th century. The notable addition is an arcade built in 1909. A couple of hundred metres along Krystalgade stands the Synagogue of Copenhagen, inaugurated in 1833.

Postal Interlude

From the Round Tower, turn left onto pleasant Købmagergade, which is one of Copenhagen's oldest commercial thoroughfares. At number 37 you'll find the **Post & Tele Museum** (Post and Telecommunications Museum; www.ptt-museum. dk; daily 10am–4pm; free). Look out for the iceboat that was used to transport mail across the Great Belt. The museum has an excellent rooftop café.

A spiral ramp winds around the inside of the Round Tower

Rosenborg Slot

Backtrack to the Round Tower and turn right, following Landemærket to its end at Copenhagen's favourite park, **Kongens Have** (King's Garden), filled with sunbathers, picnickers and families in summer. This garden was laid out in 1606–34 by Christian IV, who found Christiansborg Palace too official and oppressive. He built himself a small country mansion in a corner of the site, outside the town walls, eventually expanding it into the three-storey Dutch Renaissance-style **Rosenborg Slot** ⑭ (Rosenborg Castle; www.rosenborg slot.dk; May–Oct daily 10am–4pm, June–Aug until 5pm, Nov–Apr Tue–Sun 11am–2pm; charge). Rosenborg became home for the next three generations of kings until Frederik IV erected Frederiksberg Castle in 1710. Since 1838 it has been a royal museum of considerable grace and the home of the crown jewels.

The castle's rooms are arranged chronologically, beginning with Christian IV's tower-room study, still furnished in its original style. The Knights' Hall, with tapestries depicting Danish victories in the Swedish Wars, an ornate ceiling and three almost life-size silver lions, contains one of the world's largest collections of silver furniture, mostly from the 18th century.

The crown jewels are held in the treasury. In addition to the oldest existing insignia of the Order of the Elephant (see panel), there are 18 cases of crowns, gilded swords, precious stones and coronation cups – as well as silver boxes containing the umbilical cords of eight royal children. The centrepiece of this regal collection is the 17th-century crown of the absolute monarchy – made out of gold, diamonds, sapphires and garnets and weighing over 2kg (4lbs).

Also not to be missed is the nearby **David Collection** ⑮ (Kronprincessegade 30; www.davidmus.dk; Tue and Fri 1–5pm, Wed 10am–9pm, Thur 10am–5pm, Sat–Sun 11am–5pm;

Elephant order

The Order of the Elephant is Denmark's highest decoration. Instituted by Christian V in 1693, the insignia is worn by members of the royal family and can be bestowed upon foreign heads of state. Britain's Queen Elizabeth II is a member of the Order.

free), which has outstanding European and Islamic fine art collections.

On the other side of Rosenborg, across Øster Voldgade, visiting gardeners will be particularly interested in the newly renovated **Botanisk Have** 16 (Botanical Gardens; http://botanik.snm.ku.dk; daily May–Sept 8.30am–6pm, Oct–Apr 8.30am–4pm; free). It has Denmark's largest collection of living plants. At the time of writing, more building work was taking place in the gardens, where an ambitious plan is underway to integrate the city's zoological, botanical and geological collections into one stunning new **Natural History Museum of Denmark** (http://nyt.snm.ku.dk), to be completed by 2017.

Fine Arts Museum

Art lovers should allow themselves time to explore the **Statens Museum for Kunst** 17 (National Gallery of Denmark; Sølvgade 48–50; www.smk.dk; Tue–Sun 10am–5pm, Wed 10am–8pm; free, charge for special exhibitions), just north of the Botanical Gardens. Paintings from early Dutch to modern Danish, including a large Matisse collection and perhaps the world's finest collection of Dürer prints, are housed in a light, airy and beautifully renovated building.

Across the park at Stockholmsgade 20 is **Den Hirschsprungske Samling** (Hirschsprung Collection; www.hirschsprung.dk; Tue–Sun 11am–4pm; charge, Wed free), a delightful museum packed with 19th-century Danish painting, sculpture and decorative art. Heinrich Hirschsprung, a tobacco merchant, donated the works to the state in 1902. Look out for the portraits and landscapes of C.W. Eckersberg (1783–1853), whose meticulous style had a far-reaching influence.

It's possible to return to Rådhuspladsen by bus or by train from Nørreport Station. But, if you prefer to walk, there is another surprise: the leafy **Ørsteds Parken**, on the right-hand side of Nørre Voldgade. This charming park offers a wonderful respite during daylight hours.

NYHAVN AND BEYOND

This walk begins at Kongens Nytorv (bus 26 from Rådhuspladsen). Cross the square towards **Nyhavn** ⑱; the name literally means 'new harbour' and immediately you'll notice the nautical flavour of this former 'sailors' street', once overflowing with bars and brothels. Over the centuries the two sides of the canal have developed into a remarkable

Formal gardens around Rosenborg Slot

illustration of old Copenhagen. At the Kongens Nytorv end of the canal, which was dug in 1671 to enlarge the harbour, stands a sizeable old anchor, a memorial to the Danish sailors killed in World War II. On either side of the canal itself, an unusual collection of vessels lies at anchor with their masts colourfully bedecked with the Danish flag. This sight, combined with numerous restaurants and bars with outside terraces, and the antiques shops and other stores on the north side, draws thousands of people who are only too happy to eat, drink and socialise in such an attractive and lively setting.

This is a street with everything – history, architecture, nightlife and a constant passage of colourful small vessels. It was even home to Hans Christian Andersen, who lived here first at number 67 from 1854–64 and later at number 18.

Walk to the end of Nyhavn on the north side (with all the cafés), and you'll pass Nyhavn 71, a superb hotel conversion of an 18th-century warehouse. Just beyond is a view over the inner harbour to the Christianshavn area, where the spiralling steeple of Vor Frelsers Kirke dominates the skyline (see page 64).

Amaliehavn Gardens

Turn left down Toldbodgade to Skt Annæ Plads. This is a fine

Colourful Nyhavn

boulevard lined with consulates and distinguished old offices, with an equestrian statue of Christian X at the end overlooking Bredgade. To your right is the **Royal Danish Playhouse**  (Skuespilhuset), which opened in 2008. Cross the square, turn right and then left along the waterfront to the pleasant **Amaliehavn Gardens**. These were created by Belgian landscape architect Jean Delogne in 1983 using French limestone and Danish granite. The bronze pillars around the fountain were designed by Italian sculptor Arnaldo Pomodoro. Across the water you'll see the magnificent Opera House (see page 66).

Amalienborg Plads and Palace, home of the royal family

Amalienborg Palace

The road leading away from the water takes you to one of the most attractively symmetrical squares in Europe, **Amalienborg Plads**. A huge equestrian statue of Frederik V, 21 years in the making, dominates the centre of the square and gives you a clue that you are now in the proximity of royalty. The four (superficially) identical mansions that line the octagonal perimeter were designed by superstar 18th-century architect Nicolai Eigtved as town mansions for four noblemen. After Christiansborg Palace was destroyed by fire in 1794, the homeless royal family purchased the mansions from their aristocratic owners, and has lived here since. Today, collectively known as **Amalienborg Slot** ❷⓿ (Palace), these buildings are considered to be one of the finest rococo ensembles in Europe.

Four roads converge at right angles on the courtyard, while bearskin-clad soldiers guard each of the palaces and corners, with an extra sentry posted at the gateway between the two palaces to your left. The wing to the left of the colonnade is Christian IX's Palace, the winter residence of Queen Margrethe. On the right of the colonnade, **Christian VII's Palace** (www.ses.dk; admittance by guided tour only, in English July–Sept Sat–Sun 1pm and 2.30pm; charge) is used for receptions and to house royal guests.

Continuing around the square, the third building, Christian VIII's Palace, houses the **Amalienborg Palace Museum** (www.ses.dk; May–Oct daily 10am–4pm, Nov–Apr Tue–Sun 11am–4pm; charge), where the Royal Collection is on show in the splendid private apartments of the Danish Glücksburg kings. Among the exhibits are treasured works of art given to Christian IX (reigned 1863–1906) and Queen Louise by their six children, some of whom married into other leading European royal families. The fourth building is Frederik VIII's Palace, home to Crown Prince Frederik and his family. The name Amalienborg came from the wife of Frederik III, Queen Sophie Amalie.

The main attraction at Amalienborg when the Queen is in residence is the daily **Changing of the Guard**. At 11.30am the guards leave their barracks near Rosenborg Castle (see page 51) in formation, and march through the city streets so as to arrive in the palace square just before noon, moving from one sentry box to another in a series of foot-stamping ceremonies. Guardsmen march to the accompaniment of a band, their black bearskins rippling in the breeze. They

On duty at Amalienborg

Wartime memorabilia
at Frihedsmuseet

wear blue trousers with white stripes and highly polished boots; on festive occasions they dress in red tunics with white shoulder straps.

Churchill Park

Leave the square via Amaliegade and follow it north for about 730m to its junction with Esplanaden. Churchill Parken is on the opposite side of the road and has several interesting sights.

The **Frihedsmuseet** ㉑ (Museum of the Danish Resistance Movement 1940–45; www.natmus.dk; Tue–Sun May–Sept 10am–5pm, Oct–Apr 10am–3pm; free) is located at one of the prettiest spots in the city – especially in springtime when the daffodils are in bloom. In contrast, the museum provides a graphic record of wartime darkness and danger during the German occupation. Displays illustrate the daring exploits of the Resistance Movement.

Just beyond, the Anglican **St Alban's Church** (www.st-albans.dk) looks as if it has been transplanted from an English country village. It was indeed constructed amid the green lawns of Churchill Park in 1887 by an English architect. On a small slope next to the church there is a sight that is guaranteed to hold your attention. Copenhagen has numerous fountains but this, the **Gefion Fountain**, is the most spectacular. It was commissioned by the Carlsberg Foundation, and in 1908 sculptor Anders Bundgaard's depiction of the legend of the Nordic goddess Gefion – who turned her four sons into oxen and used them to pull the island of Zealand from Sweden – was unveiled.

The Little Mermaid

Follow the right-hand path through delightful gardens past the fountain and walk much further on to Langelinie (a waterside pier/promenade). Located just before the marina and the cruise-ship dock, near the water's edge, is Denmark's most famous statue, **Den Lille Havfrue** ㉒ (the Little Mermaid). In Andersen's fairy tale, this tragic sea-girl exchanged her voice for human legs in order to gain the love of an earthly prince, but had to watch in silence as he jilted her for a human princess. In desperation, she threw herself into the sea and turned into foam. To the dismay of both visitors and Danes, the mermaid has frequently been vandalised. Fortunately, the workshop of sculptor Edvard Eriksen retains the original moulds from 1913, and new parts can be cast if necessary. Although famous, it must be said that the statue is rather small and unassuming.

Edvard Eriksen's Little Mermaid, modelled on his wife

All quiet at the Citadel

The Citadel

After viewing the Little Mermaid, take the road running inland from the water, cross a bridge and descend the flight of steps on the left. This leads to a wooden bridge on the far side of which is **Kastellet** ㉓ (Citadel), a star-shaped fortress with five bastions. It was begun by Frederik III in 1662. Building continued until 1725 and today the fortress is still in use by the army – the church, prison and main guardhouse having resisted the assaults of time. It is a delightfully peaceful enclave, with a charming windmill (1847) and some remains of the old ramparts well worth seeing.

Leave by the wooden bridge leading south into Churchill Parken, and then turn right onto Esplanaden. Cross Store Kongensgade into Gernersgade and you are in the heart of **Nyboder** ㉔ (New Dwellings), whose long rows of houses were first built between 1631 and 1641 by Christian IV as dwellings for his sailors. More houses were built in the 18th and 19th centuries. Painted yellow-ochre, with steep gabled roofs and shuttered windows, they form a fashionable, well-preserved community of homes still inhabited by navy personnel as well as civilians. You can see what life here used to be like at **Nyboders Mindestuer** (St Pauls Gade 24; www.nybodersmindestuer.dk; Sun 11am–2pm; charge), a small museum based in the cramped rooms of two 17th-century houses.

A Stroll Along Bredgade

Backtrack to Bredgade and turn right. The area from here to Kongens Nytorv is a residential quarter of substantial granite houses and quadrangles. It was planned by architect Nicolai Eigtved at about the same time as Amalienborg. At number 68 you'll find **Designmuseum Danmark** (http://design museum.dk; Tue–Sun 11am–5pm, to 9pm Wed; charge). Housed in an attractive rococo building (a former hospital) dating from 1757, the museum focuses on Danish and European decorative art, along with Oriental handicrafts dating from the Middle Ages to the present.

On one side of the museum, at number 70, there is a plaque commemorating the death of the philosopher Søren Kierkegaard (see box) in 1855. On the other side, at number 64, is Skt Ansgars Kirke, centre of the modest Roman Catholic community since 1842. A museum documents the history

Twentieth-century design icons, Designmuseum Danmark

of Catholicism in the city since its virtual extinction in the
Reformation of 1536. Immediately after the church stands
the **Medicinsk Museion** (Bredgade 62; www.museion.
ku.dk; Wed–Fri and Sun noon–4pm; guided tours available
in English July–Aug 2.30pm; charge) – the squeamish may shy
away from its fascinating collection of medical artefacts, past
and present. Then it comes as a surprise to see, across the road,
the golden onion-shaped domes of Alexander Nevsky Kirke,
built for the Russian Orthodox community in 1883.

Marble Church

A few steps further and the great dome of the **Marmorkirken**
❷⑤ (Marble Church; www.marmorkirken.dk; Mon–Thur and
Sat 10am–5pm, Wed until 6.30pm, Fri and Sun noon–5pm;
free; visits to the dome June–Aug daily 1 and 3pm, Sept–June
Sat–Sun 1 and 3pm; charge), officially called the Frederiks
Kirken, rises high to your right. Measuring 31m (100ft) in
diameter, this is one of the largest church domes in Europe.
The cornerstone was laid by Frederik V in 1749. However, the
Norwegian marble required for the building became so expensive that the project was halted. It was eventually completed
using Danish marble and consecrated in 1894.

Søren Kierkegaard

The top-hatted figure of Søren Kierkegaard (1813–55) was a familiar
sight to Copenhageners as he took his daily walk along the city's cobbled
streets. Regarded as one of the founders of Existentialism, Kierkegaard's
philosophy developed out of personal anguish and his distaste for organised religion. You'll find a small exhibition devoted to Kierkegaard at
Københavns Bymuseum (Copenhagen City Museum; Vesterbrogade 59;
tel: 33 21 07 72; www.bymuseum.dk; daily 10am–5pm; charge, Fri free), a
ten-minute walk west from Rådhuspladsen along Vesterbrogade.

The grandiose Marble Church, modelled on St Peter's in Rome

Inside, the dome is decorated with rich frescoes in blue, gold and green, representing the Apostles. Outside, the building is surrounded by statues of personalities of the Danish Church, including St Ansgar, who helped to bring Christianity to Denmark, and Grundtvig, the 19th-century educationalist. On the roof are 16 religious figures, from Moses to Luther. Continue along Bredgade to Kongens Nytorv past an array of boutiques, antiques shops and galleries.

CHRISTIANSHAVN AND HOLMEN

Though there's so much to see within a small radius of Rådhuspladsen and Kongens Nytorv, it's worth spending a few hours across the Knippelsbro bridge in **Christianshavn**. The area was named Christian's Harbour after Christian IV, and it looks like a slice of Amsterdam, reflecting the king's predilection for Dutch architecture.

The new Opera House
at Holmen

Christians Kirke

Having crossed Knippel
Bridge you are on Torvegade.
Turn right at the intersection
with Strandgade and stroll to
the sombre **Christians Kirke**
26 (daily Mar–Oct 8am–6pm,
Nov–Feb 8am–5pm). Built in
1755 by Nicolai Eigtved, it
possesses an unexpected interior layout with three tiers
of galleries reminiscent of
an old-time music hall. The
tower was added in 1769.

Now backtrack and after crossing Torvegade continue on
Strandgade until you reach the impressive **Dansk Arkitektur**
Center (Danish Architecture Centre; www.dac.dk; daily
10am–5pm, Wed until 9pm; charge, Wed free 5–9pm), in a
former warehouse at Gammel Dok. The area has numerous 17th- and 18th-century houses with cobbled courtyards.
N.F.S. Grundtvig spent some years at number 4B. Living at
number 6 in the early 18th century was Admiral Peter Wessel
Tordenskjold – a Danish-Norwegian hero who won battles at
sea, but whose exuberant lifestyle ashore lost him many good
neighbours. It's said that every time he called *skål* (cheers) during his frequent banquets, a salute would be fired from two
cannons at the main doorway, with many a sleepless night had
by all until his death in a duel in 1720.

Vor Frelsers Kirke

Follow Skt Annæ Gade from Strandgade towards the dis-
tinctive twisted spire of **Vor Frelsers Kirke** **27** (Church of
Our Saviour; www.vorfrelserskirke.dk; tower open daily mid-
Jun to mid-Sept 10am–7pm, mid-Sept to Nov and Apr to

mid-Jun 10am–4pm, closed Dec–Mar; charge), consecrated in 1696. Its most dominant exterior feature, the dizzying staircase that twists four times around the creaking wooden tower, was designed by Lauridz de Thurah and completed in 1752. A total of 400 steps, 150 on the outside, lead from the entrance of the church to the gilt globe and Christ figure on top of the spire.

The inside of the church has many points of interest, including its choir screen, guarded by six wooden angels; the ornate white marble font supported by four cherubs; the altar dating from 1732, replete with allegorical statues and Dresden-like figures playing in the clouds; the tinkling carillon; and in particular the monumental organ, built in 1700 and several times remodelled, most recently in 1965. Beautifully ornamented, the whole construction is supported by two large stucco elephants.

Copenhagen rooftops from Vor Frelsers Kirke

A spiral staircase surrounds
Vor Frelsers Kirke tower

Christiania

Outside Vor Frelsers Kirke, turn left onto Prinsessegade and follow the brick wall to a somewhat more esoteric experience. In 1971, a group of local people broke into an abandoned military barracks here and founded **Christiania** 28 free state. Denmark proclaimed it a social experiment soon thereafter, and it has provoked controversy ever since. For many years, soft drugs were sold from stalls on the main street, although recent political pressure and police clampdowns have stopped this open sale. Around 1,000 people live and work in this community, with its eclectic collection of eateries, oddball architecture and a great concert venue, Loppen. However, as the Free Town stands on a piece of prime real-estate in a fast-growing city, it's unlikely to survive much longer – visit while you can. To get the most out of Christiania, take a guided tour (www.rundvisergruppen.dk; July–Aug daily 3pm, Sept–Jun Sat–Sun 3pm), run by local residents, departing from the main gate.

Opera House

From Christiania, continue along Prinsessegade to Holmen, where Copenhagen's dramatic modern **Opera House** 29, which opened in 2005, dominates the former docklands site on the harbour front. Designed by Danish architect Henning Larsen, the modernist Opera House is topped by a spectacular 'floating' roof. The enormous, airy foyer holds an elegant pre-show restaurant and looks like something out of *2001: A Space Odyssey*. A number of the Nordic region's most eminent artists have contributed to the interior decor, including Per Kirkeby, who created stunning bronze reliefs.

OUTLYING DISTRICTS

Although most of the main tourist attractions are clustered in and around the pretty old town, there are some gems worth seeking out in other areas of the city.

Frederiksberg

The leafy suburb of Frederiksberg (technically not part of Copenhagen, although it is surrounded by the city) is a great place for families. In summer, you can hire boats and row around the meandering canal system in rolling, romantic **Frederiksberg Have** (Frederiksberg Gardens; boats available May–Sept Mon–Fri 10am–5pm, Sat–Sun noon–6pm). Look out for the colony of tame grey herons that wander the lawns and paths close to the Chinese pavilion (May–Aug Sun 2–4pm; free; cross by the ferry boat).

From the park, there's a good view of architect Norman Foster's famous elephant house at **Zoologisk Have** (Copenhagen Zoo; Roskildevej 32; www.zoo.dk; daily July 10am–8pm, Jun and Aug 10am–6pm, Apr,

Opera house tour

Whether or not you're able to see an opera or ballet production at the city's new Opera House, a guided tour round the building is recommended – see the website www.operaen.dk for days and times and to book tickets, or tel: 33 69 69 69. The harbour bus and bus 66 serve the site.

Furnishings and decor at the Amagermuseet

May, Sept and Oct 10am–5pm, Jan–Mar and Nov–Dec 10am–4pm; charge). The zoo has lots on offer, including tigers, brown bears, polar bears and a pride of lions. If you're in the area, it's worth paying a visit to the nearby **Glass Museum** (Cisternerne – Museet for Moderne Glaskunst; www.cistern erne.dk; Mar–Oct Thu–Fri 2–6pm, Sat–Sun 11am–5pm, Nov and Feb Thu–Fri 2–5pm, Sat–Sun 11am–5pm; charge), housed in an underground water tank: glowing glass, drips of water, and crypt-like arches lend it an almost medieval atmosphere.

Also in Frederiksberg, the **Musikmuseet** ③⓪ (Danish Music Museum; Rosenørns Allé 22; www.natmus.dk), with a collection of 3,800 instruments from around the world, is due to open at the end of 2013.

Nørrebro

Nørrebro is another working-class district beginning the shift towards gentrification. **Skt Hans Torv** ③① and the surrounding streets contain some great cafés and restaurants, while interesting independent shops selling clothes and antiques are scattered along Elmegade and Ravnsborggade. It may sound odd, but one of the area's biggest attractions is **Assistens Cemetery ㉜**, where Copenhageners like to picnic, jog and play with their kids, alongside the graves of famous Danes like Hans Christian Andersen, Niels Bohr and Søren Kierkegaard.

Bispebjerg

A 25-minute journey from Rådhuspladsen on the number 6A bus brings you to the immense **Grundtvigs Kirke ㉝** (www.grundtvigskirke.dk; Mon–Sat 9am–4pm, Thur until 6pm, Sun noon–4pm; free) in the northwestern suburb of Bispebjerg. The church is a monument to N.F.S. Grundtvig (1783–1872), a renowned educationalist, austere parson and prolific hymnwriter. Built between 1921 and 1940, it is also a monument to early 20th-century Danish architecture. The church's design by Peder Jensen-Klint is simple but effective. Everything is in pale-yellow brick, from the 50m (160ft) tower to the altar.

EXCURSIONS

In a country of 44,030 sq km (16,630 sq miles), nature has ingeniously divided Denmark into a land of more than 450 islands so that you are never more than 50km (30 miles) from the sea. Copenhageners have their own beach, woodlands and wide lake area, and it is easy to organise an excursion. Options include boat trips, windmill and water-mill sightings, a visit to a royal country castle, and the chance to explore two fabulous art galleries and a couple of pretty, traditional villages.

Store Magleby and Dragør

Travellers arriving by plane will already have visited Amager island – but there are far more charming places here than

Houses from the past at the Open-Air Folk Museum

the international airport. A number 350S bus from Kongens Nytorv will take you south to the village of Store Magleby and then to charming Dragør. As many of the shops in Dragør are open on Sunday in summer, this is a good day to take the trip.

In an old farmhouse on the village street in **Store Magleby** you'll find **Amagermuseet** (Amager Museum; Hovedgaden 4 & 12; www.museumamager.dk; May–Sept Tue–Sun noon–4pm; charge). The kitchen and bedrooms are furnished in the old style with items donated by local residents representing a strong Dutch connection in the area. Christian II (1513–23) invited a colony of Netherlands farmers to improve soil cultivation in the region, and to provide the royal table with 'as many roots and onions as are needed'. He gave the Dutch special privileges to live in Store Magleby, which for centuries was referred to as Hollænderbyen (Dutchmen's Town). They had their own judicial system and church, and developed a bizarre local costume.

The lovely 18th-century village of **Dragør** ㉞, 16km (10 miles) from the city, is remarkably well preserved. A walk among the half-timbered cottages with their postage-stamp-size gardens provides a vivid impression of what life was like two or more centuries ago. Beside the boat-filled harbour, a 1682 fisherman's cottage, the oldest house in the town, has been converted into **Dragør Museum** (Havnepladsen, Strandlinien 2 & 4; www.museumamager.dk; May–Sept Tue–Sun noon–4pm; charge). It is devoted to local seafaring history.

Open-Air Folk Museum and Lyngby Lake

At Kongevejen 100, Kongens Lyngby, 16km (10 miles) north of the city, is **Frilandsmuseet** (www.natmus.dk; May to mid-Oct Tue–Sun 10am–4pm, to 5pm July; free), the intriguing Open-Air Folk Museum. The museum is accessible by car along the A3 and A5 main roads, by bus number 184 from Nørreport terminus in town, or by S-train to Sorgenfri station (leaving every 20 minutes from Copenhagen Central Station). A more interesting route is on the same train, but with a change at Jægersborg station to the little one-coach train known as *Grisen* ('The Pig'). This will drop you at Fuglevad Station near the museum's back entrance.

Over 50 farmhouses, cottages, workshops and a Dutch-type windmill are scattered about the 35-hectare (90-acre) site – all furnished in the original style, even down to combs and portraits. Broadly, the buildings are split into geographical groups laid out along country lanes, together with bridges and village pumps, and all are authentically landscaped. Each building has been transplanted, tile by tile, timber by timber, from its original location. You'll find a Zealand group, a Jutland and a Faroes group, etc. Homes of all classes are represented, from peasant to landowner, as well as artisan and farmer.

The smell of old timber and tar pervades the rooms. Geese and sheep are driven along the lanes. Displays of folk dancing, sheep shearing, threshing and weaving are given during the summer. There are horse-and-carriage rides and picnic spots in tree-lined meadows.

Allow yourself time during good weather to walk a kilometre towards **Lyngby** ㉟, where you can take a rural boat ride scarcely equalled in any capital city. On your left is the white-walled baroque castle, Sorgenfri Slot (closed to the public, although part of the gardens is accessible), built in the 18th-century by Lauridz de Thurah, who also designed the spire of Vor Frelsers Kirke (see page 64).

Proceed over Mølleåen (the Mill Stream). Follow the signs to the right for **Lyngby Sø - Bådfarten** (Lyngby Lake Boat

Calm waters in the harbour at Dragør

Trip; Sorgenfrivej 23; www. baadfarten.dk) to find two venerable canopied boats at the quayside. These have plied the four lakes since the 1890s. A 45-minute cruise, either Lyngby–Frederiksdal or Lyngby–Bagsværdvej, gives you the chance to savour the tree-covered backwaters and reedy lakes. The boats operate Tuesday to Sunday mid-June to August, weekends only May, early June and September.

Grundtvigs Kirke, an early 20th-century masterpiece

As you float by, you'll pass the 1803 mansion of Marienborg amid the trees, the official summer residence of Danish prime ministers. Further on is Frederiksdal, with its castle on a hill above. This former royal house has been lived in by the same family since 1740. An alternative trip will take you to Sophienholm Mansion (1805), now a community cultural arts centre. Outdoor café tables give an idyllic view over the waters of Bagsværd Sø.

Back on Lyngby quay, the 184 bus can take you directly back into town, or it's a short walk to Lyngby S-train station.

Arken

Søren Robert Lund was just 25 years old and a student when he won a competition to design **Arken** ㊱ (www.arken.dk; Tue–Sun 10am–5pm, Wed until 9pm; charge), to house a museum of modern art on the waterfront at Køge Bugt, 20km (12 miles) south of Copenhagen. The building gives the impression of a ship nestling in the dunes. New galleries

Kronborg, Frederik II's Renaissance castle

now allow Arken to present some of its permanent collection, which emphasises art after 1990; Damien Hirst is well represented, as he donated eight pieces to the gallery in 2011. An eclectic mix of exhibitions is also staged here throughout the year. To reach Arken, take the S-train to Ishøj (lines A or E) then walk or take bus number 128 to the museum. If you want to make a full day of it, bring your swimsuit – **Ishøj Strand**, one of the metropolitan area's best sandy beaches, is close by.

Louisiana Museum of Modern Art

If you have time for only one modern-art museum, make it **Louisiana** ㊲ (Gammel Strandvej 13, Humlebæk; www.louisiana.dk; Tue–Fri 11am–10pm, Sat–Sun 11am–6pm; charge), a 30-minute train ride from Copenhagen. The museum is a work of art in itself: the main mid-19th-century mansion is extended by whitewashed galleries built into a hilly sculpture garden, with numerous glass walls blurring the boundaries between art and nature. The extensive collection includes works by Picasso, Warhol and Rauschenberg, COBRA artists such as Asger Jorn and, more recently, Per Kirkeby. A glazed corridor leads past a group of Giacometti figures to the excellent Museum Café. Its terrace – with stunning sea views – features metal mobiles by Alexander Calder. In the gardens, you can picnic on the lawns while marvelling at Henry Moore's colossal bronze women silhouetted against the waters of the Øresund. There is an excellent range of daily children's activities, too. From Copenhagen's Central Station, take the regional train (Regionaltog) to Humlebæk, in northern Zealand, from where it's a well-signposted 1km (0.6-mile) walk from the station.

Sculpture at Louisiana

Helsingør

Further north along the coast, at the narrowest stretch of the Øresund, is Helsingør. On leaving the railway station, the town's most famous landmark comes into view – the Unesco World Heritage site **Kronborg Slot** ❸❽ (Kronborg Castle; www.kronborg.dk; June–Aug daily 10am–5.30pm, Easter–May and Sept–Oct daily 11am–4pm; Nov–Easter Tue–Sun 11am–4pm; guided tours in English 1pm, also 11am weekends and peak season; charge). To reach it on foot from the station takes about 20 minutes.

Many people will be familiar with Kronborg as 'Hamlet's castle of Elsinore'. No one knows if Shakespeare visited Kronborg personally, but some of his colleagues performed at the newly built castle, and so may have inspired him to set his tragedy here. The castle was built between 1574 and 1585 at the command of Frederik II for the purpose of extracting tolls from ships entering the narrow strait, and thus the Baltic (not a new idea – an earlier fortress on the site had also been a good money-spinner for the Danish treasury). Frederik, however, had more than just a stronghold in mind. He built a splendid Renaissance castle that could be lived in, peppered with ramparts, bastions, large windows and decorated towers. He sent for the Flemish architect Antonius van Opbergen to design the four-wing structure, then engaged various Danish and Dutch artists to paint, weave and indulge in decorative sculpture on a scale never before seen in Scandinavia.

The moated brick castle today stands as Frederik's proudest memorial, now sparsely furnished but immensely impressive. It has a feeling of solid strength and royal presence throughout, permeating the elaborate little chapel, the long galleries and stone stairways, and most of all the massive oak-beamed Great Hall – the largest of its kind in northern Europe. Decked out now with 12 paintings of the Øresund by Isaac Isaacsz, its walls were once hung with 40 tapestries by the Dutchman Hans Knieper, depicting the 113 Danish kings said to have reigned before Frederik II. Fourteen of the tapestries survive, and seven can be seen in a small room beneath the hall. Underneath the castle are extensive cellars and dungeons: you can take a tour of the cramped and creepy casemates, where the castle's besieged soldiers would have crouched in the darkness. This is also where you'll find Kronborg's most renowned exhibit, the statue of the nation's own mythical hero, Holger the Dane.

Helsingør has more to offer than the castle alone:

Holger the Dane

Legend has it that this 9th-century Viking warrior never actually died, but just went to sleep, and will wake to defend Denmark if the country is threatened. During World War II, a section of the Resistance adopted the name of Holger Danske.

there are medieval streets of colour-washed houses, the 15th-century **Skt Mariæ Kirke** and a **Carmelite Kloster** (Convent) to see, and the shiny new **M/S Maritime Museum of Denmark** (www.mfs.dk) was due to throw open its doors in the summer of 2013. A short ferry trip across the strait to colourful Helsingborg, in Sweden, is always of interest. The Helsingør tourist office (Havnepladsen 3; www.visitnorthsealand.com), near the railway station, can supply tickets, maps and information.

Mythical hero: Holger the Dane at Kronborg Slot

If you visit Helsingør on Saturday, you will come face-to-face with a social phenomenon: Swedes by the thousands making the crossing to enjoy cut-price alcohol shopping in Denmark (their own laws being strict and the prices much steeper). As a consequence, stores selling spirits, wine and beer are prevalent, and it is a strange sight to see Swedes pushing around their little two-wheeled trolleys full of booze.

Visits to Helsingør and to the Louisiana Museum of Modern Art may be readily combined. From Helsingør, board the train for Copenhagen, alighting at Humlebæk. Alternatively, at the bus terminal next to the railway station in Helsingør board a number 388 bus for the pleasant 20-minute journey along the coast to the museum. To return to Copenhagen from Louisiana turn left onto the main road to walk back to Humlebæk railway station.

Hillerød

Hillerød is the site of one of the greatest Renaissance castles in northern Europe, **Frederiksborg Slot** ❸❾ (Frederiksborg Castle; www.dnm.dk; National History Museum daily Apr–Oct 10am–5pm, Nov–Mar 11am–3pm; charge; gardens open daily 10am, closing at different hours depending on the season), sometimes called the Nordic Versailles. This dazzling brick and sandstone castle is dramatically situated across three islands on a lake, and the best way to reach it is by way of a small boat that departs from the city centre. Although the oldest parts of the castle date from around 1560 and were built by Frederik II, most of the castle dates from between 1600 and 1620 – the work of that visionary Builder King, Christian IV. The style is Dutch

Frederiksborg Slot, home to Danish monarchs for 200 years

Renaissance, and the result is spectacular. Danish monarchs resided here for about a century, and the absolute monarchs were crowned in the palace chapel from 1671.

In 1859 much of the interior was destroyed by fire, but between 1860 and 1884 it was rebuilt with financial

Karen Blixen

Rungstedlund, midway along the coast between the city and Helsingør, was home to *Out of Africa* author Karen Blixen. The house is now a museum devoted to her eventful life (www.karen-blixen.dk).

support from the brewer J.C. Jacobsen and later the Carlsberg Foundation. Since 1878 the castle has been the home of the **Danmarks Nationalhistoriske Museum** (National History Museum). This occupies more than 60 rooms and contains a complete record of the Danish monarchy, beginning with Christian I, who established the Oldenburg line (1448–1863), through all the monarchs of the following Glücksburg line to the present queen, Margrethe II. The exhibits are mostly in the form of portraits and paintings, with some pieces of period of furniture. But the rooms of the castle itself are perhaps of more interest to visitors. Riddersalen (the Knights' Hall) and the chapel are Frederiksborg's ultimate triumph. The 55m (185ft) Knights' Hall is awesome in its dimensions, with richly decorated tapestried walls, marble floor and carved wooden ceiling, all reconstructed from old drawings after the 1859 fire.

Below the Knights' Hall, Slotskirken (the chapel) escaped the fire, leaving its stunning gilt pillars and high vaulted nave virtually untouched. Almost every inch here is richly carved and ornamented. The chapel has inset black marble panels with quotations from the scriptures, marquetry panels in ebony and rare woods, and both its altar and pulpit in ebony with biblical scenes in silver relief. The organ is one of Europe's most notable, an almost unchanged original from 1610 by the Flemish master Esaias Compenius.

Roskilde Cathedral, a Unesco World Heritage Site

Around the gallery of this chapel hang the coats of arms belonging to knights of both the orders of the Elephant and the Grand Cross of Danneborg. Some modern recipients are also represented, such as Sir Winston Churchill and General Eisenhower.

Hillerød is just 9km (5 miles) from Helsingør and it is possible to visit both places in the same day (although it would make for a hurried day trip). The two towns are 30 minutes apart using the half-hourly local train (Lokalbane) service. You can travel to Hillerød from Copenhagen by S-train (on the E-line: 40-minute journey, trains every 10 minutes). Bus numbers 301, 302 and 324 go from the station to the castle.

Roskilde

According to legend, the Viking king Roar founded the town of **Roskilde** ❹⓿ around AD600. Situated 30km (19 miles) to the west of Copenhagen, this neat little town has plenty to offer those who undertake the 25-minute train journey from the capital.

Once you arrive, head straight for the centre, towards the three green spires which dominate the flat landscape. This is Roskilde's splendid **Domkirke** (Cathedral; www.roskilde

domkirke.dk; Apr–Sept Mon–Sat 9am–5pm, Sun 12.30–5pm, Oct–Mar Tue–Sat 10am–4pm, Sun 12.30–4pm; opening times can change at short notice, so check website; charge), a Unesco World Heritage site.

One of the most remarkable buildings in Denmark, it began life as a wooden church built by King Harald Bluetooth around AD1000, when he first converted to Christianity. In the 1170s, Bishop Absalon, founder of Copenhagen, built a brick-and-stone cathedral here for his new bishopric, and during the course of the next 300 years this grew into the Romanesque-Gothic amalgam of today.

Christian IV added the distinctive spires in 1635. He also erected his own burial chapel and a gilded royal pew in the north wall of the church, heavily latticed and shielded from public view so that (it is said) he could smoke his pipe in peace during Sunday services. Nearly all the Danish kings and queens since Margrete I (who died in 1412) are buried in sarcophagi and chapels all different from one another in a jumbled symphony of style.

Across the Øresund to Malmö

The opening in 2000 of the 8km (5-mile) long Øresund Bridge linking Denmark and Sweden has brought economic benefits to the communities on either side of the water and made the possibility of an excursion to Malmö all the more appealing. Founded in the mid-13th century, Malmö is Sweden's third-largest city. It has an attractive old town surrounding Stortorget, the main square. The Tourist Information Office (tel: 46 40 34 12 00; www.malmotown.com) at Malmö Central Station can supply maps and suggestions for walking routes. Trains leave Copenhagen Central Station every 20 minutes during the daytime, and hourly between 11pm and 6am. The journey takes 35 minutes.

On the south side, the chapel of King Frederik V is a simple design in white paint and Norwegian marble, with 12 tombs grouped around it. In contrast, the Christian IV chapel on the north side is marked by elaborately wrought ironwork from 1618 and interior decoration mainly from the 19th century featuring frescoes, paintings depicting scenes from his reign, and bronze statues. In 2010, the medieval St Birgitte's Chapel received a very modern glass sarcophagus, designed by Bjørn Nørgaard, which will eventually hold the present queen Margrethe and her husband.

A light note is introduced by the clock high on the south-west wall of the nave: as each hour arrives, St George and his horse rear up, beneath them a dragon utters a shrill cry, a woman figure strikes her little bell four times with a hammer and a man rings his big bell once. The chapel on the outside of the cathedral beside the north-western tower was inaugurated in 1985 and dedicated to the memory of Frederik IX, the King of Denmark from 1947–72, who is buried here.

Salvaged ship in the Vikingeskibsmuseet

To the front of the church is Stændertorvet, the traditional square of this old market town, lined with outdoor café tables in good weather, and fruit and vegetable stalls every Wednesday and Saturday morning. On Saturday there is also a popular flea market.

To the rear is parkland, where you can walk downhill through the meadow, towards the fjord and the **Vikingeskibsmuseet** (Viking Ship Museum; www.vikingeskibsmuseet.dk; mid-Jun to Aug 10am–5pm, Sept to mid-Jun 10am–4pm; charge). When 11th-century Danes wanted to block off the sea route

A chapel fit for a king at Roskilde Cathedral

to Roskilde from the marauding Norwegians, they sank five Viking ships across a narrow neck of the shallow fjord here. These ships, salvaged in 1962, now form the basis of the museum and are superbly displayed. They include a sturdy ocean-going trader and an awe-inspiring longship, the dreaded man o' war, used for long-range raiding.

The museum building stands on the edge of the water with one side made completely of glass, bringing the fjord almost into its main room. The outline of each ship was first reconstructed in metal strips, then the thousands of pieces of wood were treated and placed in position. The museum is lavishly illustrated with photographs and charts, and free film shows (in English) recount the full story of the salvage.

In recent years the Vikingeskibsmuseet has been developed into a fascinating complex in which you can see wooden boats being built by hand using the original skills, sail on one of these vessels, and eat in the attractive restaurant. Then, to end the day in a truly Viking flavour, you can sample a draught of the favourite brew of these hardy sailors, *mjød* (mead).

WHAT TO DO

SHOPPING

Shopping in Copenhagen is a quality experience, and the city's pedestrian precincts and attractive squares add to the pleasure of seeking out those special purchases. A host of interesting shops in the pleasant side streets and arcades around the Strøget area specialise in everything from antiques to avant-garde furniture, while established department stores such as Illum and Magasin du Nord offer the very best in Danish design.

VAT, or sales tax (in Danish known as MOMS), is 25 percent on all products and services. Foreign visitors who spend over 300kr in any one store displaying 'Tax-Free Shopping' stickers will be given a form so that they can reclaim the tax when they leave the country. Ask for details in the shop, or check out the websites www.taxfreeworldwide.com or www.global-blue.com.

Shopping Hours

Shopping hours vary from business to business, but general opening times are Mon–Thur 10am–6pm, Fri 10am–7pm, Sat 10am–4pm and Sun noon–4pm. A small number of shops (often food shops) are closed on Monday or Tuesday.

Certain stores stay open longer. These include bakers, florists, *smørrebrød* shops and kiosks. In addition, late-night (until 10pm or midnight) and Sunday shopping is possible at Central Station, which is like a village with a supermarket, banks open for foreign exchange, a post office, room-reservation service and snack bars.

Interior space at the Opera House

Where to Shop

Undoubtedly the place to begin is Strøget (pronounced stroy-et), a charming pedestrian-only combination of four streets starting at Rådhuspladsen with Frederiksberggade, which leads into Nygade Vimmelskaftet, Amagertorv, Østergade, and ends in Kongens Nytorv. Along Strøget, said to be the longest pedestrian-only street in the world, you will find everything you could possibly want, and much more. The finest ceramics, silver and crystal shops, superb home furnishings and interiors stores, the city's leading furriers, antiques shops, department stores, clothing shops and souvenir outlets exist harmoniously, side-by-side with a varied selection of restaurants and bars.

In the smaller streets branching off (and parallel to) Strøget is an eclectic array of music stores, potters and silversmiths, antiques shops and fashion boutiques. On the opposite side

Magasin du Nord

of Kongens Nytorv, and convenient for those visiting Amalienborg and the Marble Church, are Bredgade and Store Kongensgade. For up-and-coming designers, try bohemian Vesterbro.

Good Buys

Royal Copenhagen (www.royalcopenhagen.com) is the collective name for a group of upmarket shops located in attractive historic buildings in the heart of Strøget at numbers 4, 6, 8 and 10 Amagertorv. These are the

A hand-painted piece by Royal Copenhagen Porcelain

department store Illums Bolighus for the ultimate in modern design, home furnishings and accessories; Georg Jensen Silver; Royal Copenhagen Crystal; and the world-famous Royal Copenhagen Porcelain. The last of these, founded in 1775, uses a special underglaze technique that allows landscape pastels, and even accurate skin colours, to be reproduced. All the pieces are hand-painted after a quick first firing, then fired again for glazing at 1,400°C (2,600°F). No two pieces are alike. Fans might also want to visit the Royal Copenhagen Factory Outlet (Sondre Fasanvej 5) in the suburb of Frederiksberg, which sells cheaper end-of-lines and seconds – take the Metro to Fasanvej Station, or bus no 14 or 15.

Amber jewellery is offered everywhere, particularly in stores along Strøget. The local 'gem' (actually a fossil resin from the southern Baltic) may be cheaper here than at home, but beware, the quality can vary tremendously. Visit the House of Amber at Ravhuset, Kongens Nytorv 2.

Antiques are in plentiful supply, especially the second-hand/vintage rather than the fine-art variety. The locals flock to Bredgade, off Kongens Nytorv, and Ravnsborggade (www.ravnsborggade.dk), in the Nørrebro neighbourhood, which contains 16 antiques shops and hosts the occasional flea market.

Aquavit *(akvavit)*, the local spirit, usually flavoured with caraway seed, is cheaper than imported spirits. You'll find good prices at the airport duty-free store.

Danish furniture ranks among the world's best. Here you'll see items credited to the designer rather than to the factory. Furniture is a national pride and most good pieces will have a black circular 'Danish Furniture-Makers' sticker attached. Lamps are also lovingly designed, as are household textiles and hand-woven rugs. The best stores for sofas, chairs and tables, and the things to put on them, are: Illums Bolighus (Strøget;

Danish glassware

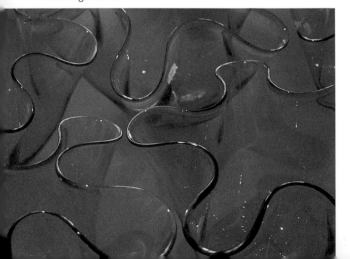

www.illumsbolighus.dk);
CasaShop (Store Regnegade
2; www.casashop.dk); Hay
Cph (Pilestræde 29-31;
www.hay.dk); Designer Zoo
(Vesterbrogade 137; www.
dzoo.dk); in Frederiksberg,
CPH Square (Carl Jacobsen

Best shopping

Check out the comprehensive shopping guides on www.aok.dk for an insider's guide to some of Copenhagen's best shopping quarters.

Vej 16; www.cphsquare.dk); and north of Osterbrø, the designer furniture store, Paustian (Kalkbrænderiløbskaj 2; www.paustian.dk).

Knitwear comes Nordic-style, often highly patterned, warm, and, in some cases, expensive. There are knitwear shops all over the city; some sell wool and patterns for those who are tempted to set about knitting their own garments.

Stereo equipment. The very latest in stereo systems, CD players, radios, and TV sets can be found at the Bang & Olufsen Centre, at Kongens Nytorv 26.

Silver is another Danish speciality, dominated by the name Georg Jensen. Silver in Denmark is quality-controlled and should always be hallmarked. The Jensen showrooms at Amagertorv 4 offer creations that range from key rings to highly precious jewellery.

Souvenirs are myriad. Little mermaid figures, Copenhagen dolls in frilly skirts and black lace caps, blue ceramic figurines and animals, and countless trolls and Vikings abound, as well as hand-painted spoons, racks and pepper mills. A particularly attractive Danish keepsake is an Amager shelf – a group of three or four small hand-painted shelves in a triangular frame that hangs on the wall. Beware, however, of cheap versions.

Toys are simple and attractive, especially those in solid wood. You'll also see hundreds of the Danish wooden soldiers in all sizes. Of course, when it comes to toys that are fun and educational, the Danish invention Lego is the daddy of them all

A new perspective on household items at furniture emporium Illums Bolighus

– their flagship store is on Strøget (Vimmelskaftet 37; www. lego.com).

Clocks and watches. Gullacksen Ure, Frederiksberggade 8 on Strøget, may not be the largest clock shop, but its owner is the third generation of an old watchmaking family. Besides a wide selection of Danish and international brand-name watches, clocks, barometers and hygrometers, look for the museum pieces on the walls. Of particular interest are the practical Jacob Jensen temperature stations.

ENTERTAINMENT

When in Copenhagen, relax as the Danes do. Rent a bike for a different view of life, walk in the beech woods and parks, have a night on the town at a concert or jazz club – or simply pause for a snack on one of the many public benches.

Nightlife

Classical music, opera, ballet. Scores of concerts are held throughout the year at the Royal Theatre, Tivoli, the Royal Conservatory of Music, Radio House, in churches and museums. Opera and ballet are performed at the splendid new Opera House – a small number of tickets are held back for sale on the day. The Royal Danish Ballet is internationally acclaimed, and rightly so – it is one of Europe's oldest, with a repertory going back 200 years. Nowadays, the company experiments in modern dance as well, but its great tradition lies in Bournonville classics, such as *La Sylphide* and *The Dancing School*. The company performs from September to June.

Clubs and bars. Copenhagen is a great place for partying. Some of Copenhagen's cosy cafés become bars at night, and many of the city's best nightspots blur the line between bar and restaurant: often when the kitchen closes, a place will slide smoothly into 'club' mode, staying open late into the night. Alcohol is expensive, so there's a tendency for people to drink at home first and start hitting the town from 11pm onwards. 'In' places come and go, but the trendy Kødbyen area in Vesterbro is the most plausible place to start: for a taste of the good life, try Karriere (Flæsketorvet 57–67; www.karrierebar.com), a place where art, design and clubbing meet. Nearby Jolene (Flæsketorvet 81–85; tel: 35 85 69 60), run by two Icelandic women, is a quirky riot. Longstanding Vega (Enghavevej 40; www.vega.dk), a huge complex containing no fewer than 12 bars, is one of the city's biggest and best mainstream clubs. There are also several

Danes entertain

If you are fortunate enough to be invited to a Danish home, don't turn down the opportunity. The Danes love to entertain and set great store by creating a cosy yet chic atmosphere for guests.

The grand interior of the Royal Theatre, built in 1874

especially friendly bars in the area around the university. Locally brewed beers are popular – sample them at BrewPub (Vestergade 29; www.brewpub.dk), near the Rådhus; or at the award-winning microbrewery Nørrebro Bryghus (Ryesgade 3; www.noerrebrobryghus.dk). Also in Nørrebro is the intimate, laid-back nightclub Rust (Guldbergsgade 8; www.rust. dk), with a minimalist, sci-fi atmosphere, which hosts top DJs and has great live shows.

Jazz, folk, rock. Copenhagen is one of Europe's leading jazz centres. The Copenhagen JazzHouse (Niels Hemmingsens Gade 10; www.jazzhouse.dk) is one of the city's premiere venues, hosting international, national and local artists. Mojo Blues Bar (Løngangsstræde 21C; www.mojo.dk) is another great live music venue that is usually packed to the brim. There's an annual 10-day Jazz Festival, which is held at the beginning of July, plus a two-week-long Vinterjazz festival at the beginning of February – the latter is countrywide, but with plenty of Copenhagen gigs. There are several venues for folk music near the university.

One of the main venues for local and international rock and pop concerts is Amager Bio (Øresundsvej 6; www.amagerbio.dk. Big names also play at Tivoli Gardens (www.tivoli.dk) and at Forum Copenhagen (www.forumcopenhagen.dk). Loppen in Christiania (www.loppen.dk) attracts a more artistic clientele, who come to see great local experimental, alternative, hardcore, world, jazz and rock shows. On summer Sundays free rock concerts are held in Fælled Park.

Cinemas. Close to Rådhuspladsen, Palads (Axeltorv 9), the Imperial (Ved Vesterport 4) and Dagmar Teatret (Jernbanegade 2) show mainstream blockbusters, and Grand Teatret (Mikkel Bryggers Gade 8) shows arthouse films. Most films are shown in their original language with Danish subtitles.

Casino. Casino Copenhagen, Radisson Hotel, 70 Amager Boulevard; tel: 33 96 59 65; www.casinocopenhagen.dk.

SPORTS

There are plenty of sporting activities to suit every taste within easy reach of the city. The top spectator sport is football (soccer), while popular participation sports include sailing and fishing. Ask the nearest Danish tourist office (see page 130) for an up-to-date list of what's available.

Cycling. Some hotels lend bicycles to their guests at no charge. Otherwise they're easy to hire (see page 119). You can use the extensive network of cycle paths *(cykelsti)* without any worry about cars, or indeed the weather–if it starts raining, country buses and trains will carry your bike and taxis have bicycle racks.

Fishing. Jutland is the Danish sea-fishing mecca, but you can still go for Øresund cod, mackerel, gar-pike, or flat-fish from

Football is Denmark's most popular spectator sport

Amager and the coast to the north of the city. A state angling licence costs 40/130/185kr per day/week/year and can be bought at campsites, fishing-tackle shops and tourist offices. You can rent licensed boats on Lyngby, Furesø and Bagsværd lakes on the northwest edge of Copenhagen.

Football. The Danish football team competes at the highest level, and the sport has an enthusiastic following. The main Copenhagen stadium is at Parken http://parken.dk, and is often used for major international matches.

Horse racing. The racetrack *(Galopbane)* at Klampenborg (www.galopbane.dk) is open mainly on Saturdays from mid-April–late October. To get there, take the regional train (Regionaltoget) RE2101 towards Helsingør, or the S-train, alighting at Klampenborg, then catch bus number 388 in the Lyngby direction.

Kayaking. Guided kayaking tours of Copenhagen harbour and Christianshavn's canals are available from Kayakole, tel:

40 50 40 06, www.kajakole.com; also kayak polo at Amager Strandpark.

Sailing. Join enthusiasts sailing on the Øresund and inland lakes. Yachts and cruisers are available for hire. Evidence of navigational proficiency is required for sailing on the Øresund, where the constant ferry traffic needs experience. Book in advance with help from your local Danish tourist office (see page 130).

Skating. Numerous stretches of water within the capital's boundaries freeze up in winter and outdoor rinks (*skøjtebaner*) are set up in the city centre, such as at Frederiksberg Runddel and Kongens Nytorv.

Swimming. There is good sea bathing along the Zealand coast north and south of Copenhagen, but the sea is rarely warm. Nude bathing is mainly at Tisvildeleje, away from the north coast. There are about a dozen indoor swimming pools in Copenhagen, some with sauna/massage and gym facilities, and several outdoor pools which are open from mid-May until the end of August. So successful has the clean-up of the Inner Harbour been that there is now a fantastically popular outdoor swimming pool at Islands Brygge (open June–Aug 7am–7pm), with diving towers and a green lawn full of picnickers in front. There are plans to create saunas and thermal baths so the area can open year-round. Another wonderful facility is Amager Strandpark (www.amager-strand.dk), a vast man-made beach and lagoon just 5km (3 miles) from the city centre, where Copenhageners flock to swim, run, skate, and play beach volleyball. There are Metro stations at three places along the beach: Øresund, Amager Strand and Femøren.

Watersports. Water-skiing is popular on the Furesø, and it is possible to windsurf in Vedbæk harbour – consult the tourist office for details. At Amager Strandpark (see above), you can rent kayaks from Kajakhotellet (http://kajakhotellet.

Main hall at the Experimentarium Science Centre

dk) or learn to kite-surf with KiteCPH (www.kitecph.dk).

CHILDREN'S COPENHAGEN

Amusement parks. Tivoli (see page 27) should certainly appeal to the entire family. Less well known than Tivoli – and generally considered to be a rather downmarket version – is Bakken (tel: 39 63 35 44; www.bakken.dk), which is extremely popular with Danes. Situated on the outskirts of Klampenborg, just a 12-minute train ride from the centre of Copenhagen, it has 33 rides, 40 cafés and restaurants and the country's most famous revue show. Entry to the park is free, and an all-ride pass costs 249kr.

Museums and attractions. Ripley's Believe it or Not Museum (Rådhuspladsen 57; tel: 33 32 31 31; www.ripleys. com/copenhagen) houses a collection of 'bizarre but true' exhibits. The Experimentarium Science Centre (Tuborg Havnevej 7; tel: 39 27 33 33; www.experimentarium.dk) is a lively place where children are positively encouraged to tinker around with exhibits. The Frilandsmuseet (see page 71) always goes down well with kids. At Christiansborg children can visit the Royal Stables (see page 41) and see the coaches and the horses that pull them.

Several major museums have special sections for children. These include the Nationalmuseet (see page 45), Statens Museum for Kunst (see page 52) and Louisiana (see page 74). The Royal Danish Naval Museum (Orlogsmuseet; Overgaden Oven Vandet 58; tel: 33 11 60 37; www.orlogsmuseet.dk) features a magnificent display of model ships, a children's playroom and a replica submarine into which kids can climb. The Viking Ship Museum at Roskilde (see page 83) has a children's section where two Viking ships may be boarded.

Copenhagen's Zoologisk Have (see page 67), established more than 120 years ago, is a good place to spend an afternoon. It houses more than 2,500 animals and has a fine children's section, restaurant and cafeteria. Den Blå Planet (The Blue Planet; Jacob Fortlingsvej 1, 2770 Kastrup; tel: 44 22 22 44; www.denblaaplanet.dk) opened in 2013 in an amazing new swirl-shaped building on Amager Island (visible as you're coming in to land at the international airport). The aquarium, a 200m walk from Kastrup Metro station, contains over 17,000 animals, including piranha, sharks, sea lions and anacondas.

Swimming. Indoors, Vandkulturhuset at the DGI sports centre (Tietgensgade 65; tel: 33 29 80 00; www.dgi-byen.dk) is a state-of the-art swimming complex with facilities for children of all ages. Outdoors, the Islands Brygge harbour swimming pool (see page 95) has two children's sections.

Entertainer at Bakken

Tours. Canal trips are a must (see page 123). Worth considering are boat cruises, such as those from Lyngby (see page 72).

Calendar of Events

Most of Copenhagen's annual festivals involve music. For an up-to-the-minute guide to what's on, visit the Copenhagen Visitor Centre (see page 130) or pick up a copy of *Copenhagen This Week*.

February Vinterjazz: two weeks of winter jazz. Frost Festival: a month of pop/electronic gigs in unusual venues around the city.

Shrovetide Beating the Barrel, parades and carnival festivities, centred around Rådhuspladsen and the Nationalmuseet. Also at Dragør on Amager island.

April Queen's birthday (16 April): crowds gather outside Amalienborg Slot at noon for the Queen's balcony appearance. CPH PIX: 10-day international film festival.

May Marches and brass bands converge on Fælled Park on May Day. Copenhagen Marathon held in mid-May. Distortion: 90,000 ravers join a citywide party (late May/early June).

Whitsuntide Copenhagen Carnival: colourful Latin-style processions and hundreds of bands attract large numbers of spectators.

June St Hans Eve (23 June): bonfires burn to celebrate the longest day. Roskilde Festival (late June): Denmark's biggest rock festival.

July Copenhagen Jazz Festival: bands play every jazz style from bebop onwards, on stage, in pubs and on the streets.

August Copenhagen Historic Grand Prix: vintage cars take to the streets. Ballet Festival: performances by the Royal Danish Ballet. Copenhagen Pride: five-day LGBT event culminating in a colourful parade. Kulturhavn: harbour-based festival, with music, dancing and family fun.

September Golden Days Festival: celebrates a different era of Copenhagen's history each year with all manner of cultural events. Blues Festival: concerts at venues across the city.

October Night of Culture: museums, galleries, churches, libraries and theatres open their doors after dark and invite the public inside. Mix Copenhagen: gay and lesbian film festival.

November–December Tivoli is transformed into a winter wonderland with glittering illuminations, ice-skating and a Christmas market.

EATING OUT

Food is of a high standard in Denmark, and is a national obsession. Danes at home will happily spend two hours over their *frokost* (lunch) or up to four hours if entertaining special guests, while a celebratory *middag* (dinner) can last from 6pm to very, very late. This leisurely style of dining carries over into the cosy, welcoming café culture: sit as long as you like over a beer or coffee, and take time out to meet the Danes.

Restaurants and Bars

There are more than 2,000 restaurants, cafés, bars and snack bars in Copenhagen. Restaurants often serve a special dish of the day *(dagens ret)* and what is known as the *dan-menu* – a two-course Danish lunch or dinner for a fixed price – in addition to *à la carte* items. Keep an eye open for a *daglig kort* (daily menu), which usually features less-expensive dishes than those listed on the more formal menu *(spisekort)*. You'll also find little lunch-only, cosy cellar restaurants listed in *Copenhagen This Week* (see page 126). These offer good value with an old-world charm, and are frequented by Danes

Alfresco dining on Nyhavn

themselves. Copenhagen has more than its fair share of fine restaurants, 13 of which have been awarded Michelin stars (Noma, named as the world's best by Restaurant magazine, boasts two). For a drink, drop into one of the numerous cafés, pubs or bars dotted throughout the city.

Most restaurants stop serving at 9 or 10pm, and many close on Sunday/Monday. A charge is often made for using foreign credit cards. VAT and service charges are included in the bill. Danes are not tip-minded, although after a meal you may want to round up your bill. At very good restaurants, after excellent service, show your appreciation with up to a 5 percent tip.

Breakfast

Breakfast *(morgenmad)* in a Danish hotel is a far cry from the Spartan 'continental breakfast' of a roll and a cup of coffee. Bread rolls, cold cuts, cheeses, jam, pastries and probably eggs are all accompanied by milk and fruit juice followed by tea or coffee.

Cold Dishes

Cold food is Denmark's truly outstanding culinary speciality. *Smørrebrød* (open sandwiches) are thickly buttered slices of heavy Danish rye bread covered with one of a wide array of delicacies: liver pâté *(leverpostej)*, veal *(kalvekød)*, ham *(skinke)*, roast beef *(stegt oksekød)*, salmon *(laks)*, smoked eel *(røget ål)*, shrimp *(reje)*, cod roe *(torskerogn)*, pickled herring *(sild)*, a variety of salads *(salat)* or cheese *(ost)*. This main layer is garnished with various accessories that have been carefully chosen to enhance both taste and appearance.

Larger restaurants have scores of different *smørrebrød*. The usual procedure is to mark your orders on the menu itself, specifying which kind of bread you want (*knækbrød*: crispbread; *rugbrød*: rye; *franskbrød*: white; or *pumpernikkel*: black).

Don't confuse your *smørrebrød* with the Swedish word *smorgasbord*. The famous Scandinavian buffet-style spread is known in Denmark as *det store kolde bord* (the cold table), and usually offers a bewildering array of dishes. For a fixed price, you start at one end of the table, helping yourself to herring in various forms, seafood, salads and other delicacies, and go on to sample liver pâté, ham and other cuts of meat. Despite its name, the cold table always includes hot items, such as meatballs, pork sausages, soup and fried potatoes. Several kinds of bread and salads are also provided. Danish *akvavit* (see page 105) and beer go especially well with *koldt bord.*

Fish and Shellfish

Fish (or small canapés) is the traditional first course of a full meal. It is also available as a main course, and a great variety of fish appears on the Danish menu. Herring is one of the firm favourites, and may be served pickled or fried, with a sherry, vinegar, curry or fennel dressing. Succulent red Greenland

Copenhagen's restaurants offer a wide choice of seafood dishes

shrimps are also popular. Lobster is also offered – though it is not cheap – as is crab, cod and halibut. Plaice features frequently in the local cuisine and may be served boiled or fried with a garnish of shellfish or parsley.

One great Scandinavian delicacy is *gravad laks*, in which raw salmon is pressed with salt and a small amount of sugar, and then sprinkled generously with chopped dill. A creamy sauce of oil, mustard and sugar is traditionally served alongside as an accompaniment.

Meat and Poultry

Although Danish meat dishes most frequently make use of pork and veal, beef has made a major breakthrough, as Danish farmers now breed more cattle. The kinds of steak that you are most likely to be offered are *fransk bøf* (fillet steak served with herb butter and French fries) and *engelsk bøf* (fillet steak served with fried onions and potatoes).

The top restaurants cook in classic French/international style. In small establishments, some typical Danish hot dishes appear on the menu such as *mørbradbøf*, a delectable legacy of the pork-only days – small cuts of tenderloin, lean, very tasty and served as a main course with boiled potatoes, onions and gravy.

More ordinary fare – but delicious nevertheless – are Danish meatballs (*frikadeller*), a finely minced mixture of pork and veal, often served with potato salad and red cabbage. *Biksemad* is also cheap and tasty: a Danish hash of diced potatoes, meat and onions with a fried egg on top. A hearty Danish stew is *Hvids labskovs*, made from chunks of beef boiled with potatoes, peppercorns and bay leaves.

Summer shrimps

A summer seafood speciality is *danske rejer*, small pink shrimps from local waters that are served piled high on white bread.

Chicken is most often served roasted with potatoes fried in butter and a cucumber salad (*agurkesalat*). Roast duck

Stalls filled with fresh produce in a city market

is served with apple or prune stuffing and is usually accompanied by caramelised potatoes and a generous array of vegetables.

Salads

The word for salad, *salat*, has two meanings. It can be a side dish of fresh lettuce, tomato, sliced egg and plentiful red peppers; or, more often, it's one of several mayonnaise mixtures, which are eaten on *smørrebrød* or as an appetiser. *Italiensk salat* consists of carrots, asparagus, peas and macaroni. *Skinkesalat* is basically chopped ham; *sildesalat* comprises marinated or pickled herring, beetroot and apple. These are the most common of the many sandwich salads available.

Cheese and Fruit

Danish Blue *(Danablue)*, a rich, sharp-flavoured cheese, has always had a strong international following, along with Havarti. Fynbo and Samsø, both relatively mild and firm

Drinks in the sunshine

cheeses, possess a sweet, almost nutty flavour. *Rygeost*, smoked cream cheese spiced with cumin seed, is wonderful.

Desserts

You will have gathered that Denmark is not a good place for dieting. And by the time you get to the desserts your best intentions will have been quite definitely routed. Desserts are usually laced with cream (*fløde*) or whipped cream (*flødeskum*). Favourites include: *æblekage* (stewed apples with vanilla, served with alternating layers of biscuit crumbs and topped with whipped cream) and *bondepige med slør* (a mixture of rye-bread crumbs, stewed apple, sugar and the ubiquitous whipped cream).

Snacks

For a snack with a difference, try the deep-fried Camembert cheese served with toast and strawberry jam (*ristet franskbrød med friturestegt camembert og jordbærsyltetøj).* The university area is good for cheap goulashes, hashes, chicken and *hånd-madder* (usually three slender *smørrebrød* with different toppings). Hot-dog stands *(pølsevogn)* are found everywhere, serving red Danish sausages *(pølse)* with mustards and relishes.

Curiously, Danish pastry is known here as Viennese pastry *(wienerbrød).* This light and flaky delight can be found in any *konditori* (bakery), and makes a delectable snack.

Drinks

Golden Danish lager comes in several types: *lys pilsner* (light lager), which has only 2 percent alcohol; the more normal green-bottle pilsner; and the stouts and special beers (such as Carlsberg Elephant) at 6 to 7 percent or more. Pilsner is available everywhere almost 24 hours a day. In addition, more diverse beers have become available recently, with excellent microbrews and imported European beers widely sold.

Akvavit is fiery Danish schnapps made from potatoes, often with a caraway taste. The colour varies according to the herbs and spices that have been used for flavouring. It is sipped at mealtimes during the opening fish course or with

Skål! ...and tak!

Learn to say *skål* (the vowel is between 'loll' and 'hall') with your beer or *akvavit.* It's more than just Danish for 'cheers', it's a ritual if you are invited to a Danish home. Your host usually has the privilege of making the first toast, and will raise a glass, point it towards everyone in turn, looking directly at them, and say 'skål'. After all have taken a sip or a swallow, the host will look at each again in turn before putting down the glass.

After the meal itself, the appropriate – and essential – words to say are *'tak for mad'* (pronounced *'tak for maad'*), meaning, very simply, 'thanks for the meal'.

the cheese, and will sometimes be washed down with a beer chaser. If you order *akvavit* with your meal, the bottle may occasionally be put on the table for you to help yourself. Don't be deluded into thinking you'll only be charged for a single measure – back at the bar they'll know exactly how much has gone.

All wines are imported and while there is a wide selection of French, German and Italian varieties, they are always expensive in restaurants. Even cheap house wine (*husets vin*) may be three times the supermarket price. After your dinner, try the Danish cherry liqueur, *Cherry Heering*.

Coffee (*kaffe*) can be found everywhere – rich, strong and served with cream. The price may seem high, but the waiter will usually come around offering refills. On a chilly day you might like to try *varm kakao med flødeskum* – a hot cocoa with whipped cream.

Carlsberg, brewed in the capital

TO HELP YOU ORDER ...

Could we have a table? **Kan vi få et bord?**

Do you have a set menu? **Har De en fast menu?**

I'd like a/an/some ... **Jeg vil gerne have ...**

beer **en øl**	napkin **en serviet**
bread **brød**	pepper **peber**
coffee **kaffe**	potatoes **kartofler**
dessert **en dessert**	salad **en salat**
fish **fisk**	salt **salt**
glass **et glas**	soup **suppe**
ice cream **is**	sugar **sukker**
meat **kød**	tea **te**
menu **et spisekort**	vegetables **grønsager**
milk **mælk**	(iced) water **(is) vand**
mustard **sennep**	wine **vin**

...AND READ THE MENU

agurkesalat cucumber salad	**kylling** chicken
blomkål cauliflower	**kål** cabbage
citron lemon	**lagkage** layer cake
flæskesteg roast pork and crackling	**lever** liver
grøn peber green pepper	**løg** onion
grønne bønner French beans	**medisterpølse** pork sausage
gulerødder carrots	**nyre** kidney
hamburgerryg loin of pork	**oksekød** beef
hindbær raspberry	**pommes frites** French fries
jordbær strawberry	**porre** leek
kartoffelmos mashed potatoes	**rødkål** red cabbage
kirsebær cherry	**ssvinekød** pork
kotelet chop	**øtunge** sole
	æble apple
	æg egg
	æggekage omelette

PLACES TO EAT

The restaurant prices in this section are based on the cost of an average three-course evening meal (set menu) for one person, including tax but excluding drinks.

$$$$ over 600kr $$$ 400–600kr
$$ 250–400kr $ below 250kr

AROUND RÅDHUSPLADSEN AND VESTERBRO

A Hereford Beefstouw $$$ *by Tivoli, Vesterbrogade 3, DK-1620 Copenhagen V; tel: 33 12 74 41; www.a-h-b.dk.* Juicy steaks are cooked to order here. It's a restaurant chain with a difference – a percentage of the profits are invested in the quality art that adorns the restaurants. Open daily 11.30am–4pm and 5–10.30pm.

Andersen Bakery $ *Bernstorffsgade 5, DK-1677 Copenhagen V; tel: 33 75 07 35; www.andersen-danmark.dk.* Excellent bakery with a Tivoli café attached: stop in for a light lunch or to try one of their renowned gourmet hot dogs. Open Mon–Fri 6.30am-7pm, Sat–Sun 7.30am–7pm.

Bang & Jensen $ *Istedgade 130, DK-1650 Copenhagen V; tel: 33 25 53 18; http://blog.bangogjensen.dk.* A chilled-out café-bar with a bohemian vibe, Bang & Jensen is perfect for everything from breakfast to a late-night beer. There's a small menu of light home-made meals, including sandwiches, chilli con carne, pasta and baba ganoush. Open Mon–Fri 7.30am–2am, Sat 10am–2am, Sun 10am–midnight.

BioMio $$ *Halmtorvet 19, DK-1700 Copenhagen V; tel: 33 31 20 00; http://biomio.dk.* In Copenhagen's on-trend Meatpacking District, BioMio serves healthy organic food with touches of the Far East to meat-eaters and veggies. Order your food directly from the chef in the open kitchen, and dine at sociable communal tables. Open Mon–Fri noon–11pm, Sat–Sun 11am–11pm.

Formel B $$$$ *Vesterbrogade 182, DK-1800 Frederiksberg C; tel: 33 25 10 66; www.formel-b.dk.* This Michelin-starred restaurant offers an impeccable gastronomic experience. Classical French cooking is honed with Danish raw materials inspired by the modern European kitchen. Set menu. Open Mon–Sat 5.30pm–10pm.

Kodbyens Fiskebar $$ *Flæsketorvet 100, DK-1711 Copenhagen V; tel: 32 15 56 56; http://fiskebaren.dk.* This popular place in the Meatpacking District shows off Scandinavia's fish and seafood to great effect – think sea urchins from Norway, Limfjorden oysters, char from lake Vättern. If you don't have a restaurant reservation, you might get a seat at the bar. Open Tue–Sat from 5.30pm.

Mother $ *Høkerboderne 9-15, DK-1712 Copenhagen V; tel: 22 27 58 98; www.mother.dk.* You'll pay premium prices to dine in cool Kødbyen, but Mother is one of the best-value restaurants in the area, serving scrumptious sourdough pizzas to hungry crowds. Reservations are taken only up to 8pm, then it's a free-for-all. Open Sun–Wed 11am–11pm, Thur–Sat 11am–1am.

Nimb $$–$$$$ *Berstorffsgade 5, DK-1577, Copenhagen V; tel: 88 70 00 00; www.nimb.dk.* The wonderful Moorish Palace in Tivoli contains two smart bars and three top-rated restaurants: the family-friendly brasserie, the Bar'n'Grill, and the Terrace, a French-inspired bistro.

PatéPaté $$–$$$ *Slagterboderne 1, DK-1716 Copenhagen V; tel: 39 69 55 57; http://patepate.dk.* Fashionable yet friendly, this relaxed restaurant in the hip Kødbyen district serves up delicious French, Spanish and Moroccan food at big shared tables. With its candle-lit bistro feel and huge wine list, it really comes into its own at night. Open Mon–Sat 9am to at least midnight.

Rio Bravo $–$$ *Vester Voldgade 86, DK-1552 Copenhagen V; tel: 33 11 75 87; www.riobravo.dk.* A no-nonsense cowboy-style steakhouse, where even the seats at the bar are saddles. A popular place with Copenhagen's late-night revellers. Open Mon–Sat 11.30am–5am, Sun 5pm–5am.

Trois Cochons $$ *Værnedamsvej 10, DK-1619 Copenhagen V; tel: 33 31 70 55; www.cofoco.dk.* On the edge of Vesterbro and Frederiksberg, this place is worth the walk for the combination of good-value food, attractive surroundings and its position on Copenhagen's self-confessed foodie street. Housed in an old butcher's shop, it serves up gourmet, hearty French bistro food amongst candles, chandeliers and glass-panelled cabinets. Open Mon–Sat noon–2.30pm, 5.30pm–midnight, Sun 5.30pm–midnight.

STRØGET AND BEYOND

Restaurant L'Alsace $$ *Ny Østergade 9/Pistolstræde, DK-1101, Copenhagen K; tel: 33 14 57 43; www.alsace.dk.* Looking out onto a charming courtyard surrounded by 17th-century buildings, this restaurant has an interesting and diverse menu. Specialities include Iberian ham, oysters, caviar and other seafood. Open Mon–Sat 11.30am–midnight.

Café Sorgenfri $ *Brolæggerstræde 8, DK-1211 Copenhagen K; tel: 33 11 58 80; www.cafesorgenfri.dk.* In a central location just south of Strøget, this Danish diner serves *smørrebrød* and classic dishes below ground level and has a good reputation. Mon–Sat 11am–11pm, Sun noon–6pm.

Frankie's Køkken $$ *Admiralgade 25, DK-1066 Copenhagen K; tel: 33 13 33 77; www.bistrobooking.dk/frankies.* Well-made food with a faintly experimental air is served in this cellar restaurant, on a quaint little street in the old town. A small menu of meat-and-fish mains is served up on charmingly mismatched plates. Open Mon–Sat 5.30–10pm

House of Souls $$–$$$ *Vestergade 3, DK-1456 Copenhagen K; tel: 33 91 11 81; http://houseofsouls.wordpress.com.* If you grow weary of *smørrebrød* and *stegt flæsk*, a plateful of Caribbean soul food might give you the spice you're seeking. Tasty and unusual dishes include Voodoo Beef, coconut pesto bread, seafood jambalaya and Creole lime mousse. Just off Gammeltorv. Open daily from 5.30pm.

Kanal Caféen $ *Frederiksholms Kanal 18, DK-1220 Copenhagen K; tel: 33 11 57 70; www.kanalcafeen.dk.* Enjoy a smørrebrød in a maritime atmosphere at this excellent Danish lunch restaurant. Step down from street level into a warren of cosy rooms, and feast on herring, meatballs and smoked salmon from Bornholm. Open Mon–Fri 11.30am–5pm, Sat 11.30am–3pm.

Københavner Caféen $–$$ *Badstuestræde 10, DK-1209 Copenhagen K; tel: 33 32 80 81; http://kobenhavnercafeen.dk.* Handily situated just off Strøget, heading south in the direction of Gammel Strand, this place is particularly recommended for its Danish cold table and the daily Copenhagen Plate, which offers seven items for a very reasonable set price. Open daily 11am–midnight.

Kong Hans Kælder $$$$ *Vingaardsstræde 6, DK-1070 Copenhagen K; tel: 33 11 68 68; www.konghans.dk.* This lovely cellar restaurant, with its swooping Gothic arches and Michelin star, is one of Denmark's finest. It serves cuisine based on classical French dishes, freshened with new ingredients. There's a very fine wine list, and it has its own salmon smokehouse. Open Mon–Sat 6pm–midnight.

Krogs Fiskerestaurant $$–$$$ *Gammel Strand 38, DK-1202 Copenhagen K; tel: 33 15 89 15; www.krogs.dk.* In an 18th-century building with early-20th-century decor, this classic restaurant is justly renowned for its excellent fish dishes. Reservations are recommended. Open Mon–Sat lunch and dinner.

Madklubben $ *Store Kongensgade 66, DK-1264 Copenhagen K; tel: 33 32 32 34; www.madklubben.info.* A riposte to the high-falutin' side of the Copenhagen dining scene, Madklubben is an unpretentious place that serves fabulous food, but keeps costs low by offering a short-and-simple menu with surcharges for more expensive dishes. Near the Marble Church. Open Mon–Sat 5.30pm–10pm.

RizRaz $ *Kompagnistræde 20, DK-1208 Copenhagen K (also at Kanikkestræde 19); tel: 33 15 05 75; www.rizraz.dk.* RizRaz does a splendid Mediterranean vegetarian buffet (spinach lasagne, falafel, tabouleh etc) for 79kr at lunch, 99kr in the evening; meat-eaters can sink their canines into a burger. Heaps of tasty food for budget travellers. Open daily 11.30am–midnight.

Slotskælderen hos Gitte Kik $–$$ *Fortunstræde 4, DK-1065 Copenhagen K; tel: 33 11 15 37; www.slotskaelderen.dk.* Come to this delightful traditional lunch restaurant to feast on *smørrebrød*, served in a cosy basement. Open Tue–Sat 10am–5pm.

Tight $$ *Hyskenstræde 10, 1207 Copenhagen K; tel: 33 11 09 00; www.tight-cph.dk.* This classy and comfortable café-restaurant presents a small but carefully chosen selection of dishes from around the world – and every one is a winner, from the truffley mushroom soup to the sticky-toffee pudding. Open Mon–Fri 5pm–10pm, Sat–Sun noon–10pm.

UNIVERSITY QUARTER AND PARKS

Café & Ølhalle 1892 $–$$ *Rømersgade 22, DK-2200 Copenhagen N; tel: 33 33 00 18; www.arbejdermuseet.dk.* This 'Café and Beer Hall' is part of Arbejdermuseet (the Workers' Museum) and offers traditional Danish grub served in an authentic 19th-century atmosphere. It also serves unique beers and aquavit, created especially for the museum by the Braunstein microbrewery. Open daily 11am–5pm.

Det Lille Apotek $$ *Store Kannikestræde 15, DK-1169 Copenhagen K; tel: 33 12 56 06; www.detlilleapotek.dk.* Just a short walk from the Round Tower, 'The Little Pharmacy' is Copenhagen's oldest restaurant – Hans Christian Andersen is said to have dined here. It serves delicious Danish food – try the deluxe lunch-plate selection, or the juicy roast pork with crackling. Open daily 11.30am–10pm.

Firefly $ *Frederiksborggade 26, DK-1360 Copenhagen K; tel: 33 36 33 30; http://fireflygarden.com.* Near the Botanical Gardens, Firefly is a raw food / vegetarian café-restaurant (currently the only 100-percent meat-free place in town). Its changing menu and delicious cocktails makes use of seasonal organic produce. Open Mon–Sat 11.30am–10pm, Sun 11.30am–4pm.

Geranium $$$$ *Per Henrik Lings All 4, DK-2100 Copenhagen Ø; tel: 69 96 00 20; www.geranium.dk.* This Michelin-starred restaurant has a strange location, on the 8th floor of the national football stadium, Parken. Very much in the Noma vein, the food is organic, seasonal and biodynamic. Open Wed dinner, Thur–Sat lunch and dinner.

Restaurant Godt $$$$ *Gothersgade 38, DK-1123 Copenhagen K; tel: 33 15 21 22; www.restaurant-godt.dk.* 'Godt' means good, which is an understatement for this small, family-run 20-seat restaurant. The cuisine is European with one daily four-course menu and a mainly French, though expanding, wine list. Open Tue–Sat dinner.

Orangeriet $$–$$$ *Kronprinsessegade 13, DK-1306 Copenhagen K; tel: 33 11 13 07; www.restaurant-orangeriet.dk.* The setting makes this restaurant – its terrace and bank of windows look out over the beautiful Kongens Have gardens. It's pricey, but on a summer's day, it's a winner for a traditional *smørrebrød* lunch. Open Mon–Sat 11am–midnight, Sun noon–4pm.

Peder Oxe $$ *Gråbrødretorv 11, DK-1154 Copenhagen K; tel: 33 11 00 77; www.pederoxe.dk.* Danish and French cuisine is served at Peder Oxe, one of a number of fine restaurants on this attractive square. Outdoor seating, great salad bar, good wine list. Open daily 11.30am–10.30pm.

Restaurationen $$$$ *Møntergade 19, DK-1116 Copenhagen K; tel: 33 14 94 95; www.restaurationen.com.* A charismatic restaurant close to the Round Tower, very much reflecting the personalities of the owners, Bo and Lisbeth Jacobsen. One fixed-price menu, featuring seasonal produce, which is changed weekly. Open Tue–Sat dinner; closed July.

NYHAVN AND BEYOND

Restaurant BioM $$ *Fredericiagade 78, DK-1310 Copenhagen K; tel: 33 32 24 66; www.biom.dk.* BioM uses only the finest organic ingredients to prepare its modern Danish menu. It's particularly fab for Saturday brunch, served until 2pm. Just a few minutes' walk from Amalienborg Palace, with views of Nyboder. Open Tue–Sat 11.30am–11pm.

Els $$ *Store Strandstræde 3, DK-1255 Copenhagen K; tel: 33 14 13 41; www.restaurant-els.dk.* The elegant 19th-century decor of this delightful restaurant close to Kongens Nytorv complements the stylish cuisine. Fish is a speciality, and the menu changes with the seasons. Reservations are strongly advised. Open daily 11.30am–10.30pm.

Ida Davidsen $–$$ *Store Kongensgade 70, DK-1274 Copenhagen K; tel: 33 91 36 55; www.idadavidsen.dk.* This family-run concern in Frederiksstaden serves a staggering 250 types of *smørrebrød*, with a choice of differently flavoured *akvavit* (Danish schnapps) to accompany them. The decor is traditional. Arrive in good time to secure a table for lunch. Highly recommended. Open Mon–Fri 10.30am–4pm.

Lumskebugten $$$ *Esplanaden 21, DK-1263 Copenhagen K; tel: 33 15 60 29; www.lumskebugten.dk.* A small and exclusive restaurant by Churchill Park near the Little Mermaid statue, with fine food and fine wine. Vegetarians can delight in their own three-course menu – a joy in such a meat-and-fish-oriented city. Reservations are essential. Open Mon–Tue lunch, Wed–Sat lunch and dinner.

Nyhavns Færgekro $$ *Nyhavn 5, DK-1051 Copenhagen K; tel: 33 15 15 88; www.nyhavnsfaergekro.dk.* An unpretentious restaurant serving particularly good traditional food. It's renowned for its all-you-can-eat herring buffet (119kr), with the fish prepared in 10 different ways. The location alongside Nyhavn is wonderful; you can choose to sit inside or outside depending on the weather. Open daily 11am–10pm.

Pastis $$ *Gothersgade 52, DK-1264 Copenhagen K; tel: 33 93 44 11; www.bistro-pastis.dk.* Locals rate this brasserie, near Kongens Nytorv, for its cosy ambiance and concise menu of fiercely French favourites – snails, *lapin Provençale*, bouillabaisse. The set menu is good value for this standard of cooking. Open Mon–Sat 11am–10.30pm.

Restaurant Rasmus Oubæk $$$ *Store Kongensgade 52, DK-1264 Copenhagen K; tel: 33 32 32 09; www.rasmusoubaek.dk.* An excellent French brasserie, serving hearty soups, steaks and pies full of flavour. Dishes are small, with two forming one course, so your taste buds get twice the delight! Open Mon–Fri lunch and dinner, Sat dinner.

Le Sommelier $$$ *Bredgade 63-65, DK-1260 Copenhagen K; tel: 33 11 45 15; www.lesommelier.dk.* French in name and French in style, with a large bar and dining area. Forty wines by the glass and 1,400 in the cellar. Open Mon–Fri lunch and dinner, Sat–Sun dinner.

Zeleste $$ *Store Strandstræde 6, DK-1255 Copenhagen K; tel: 33 16 06 06; www.zeleste.dk.* This delightful little restaurant is tucked away just off Nyhavn, but you won't miss it as long as they continue to hang a great big kitsch shrimp outside. In summer eat out in the courtyard; in winter, the small traditional rooms are appealingly cosy. They specialise in seafood and hearty meat dishes, such as rack of lamb or Argentine striploin. Open daily 11am–10pm.

CHRISTIANSHAVN AND HOLMEN

Era Ora $$$$ *Overgaden Neden Vandet 33B, DK-1414 Copenhagen K; tel: 32 54 06 93; www.era-ora.dk.* Opened in 1983, this Michelin-starred restaurant offers innovative gourmet Italian cuisine. Lunch menus are 3, 4 or 5 courses, while the evening dining experience takes you on a 'journey' of inventive and surprising courses – a short trip is 800kr, while the longest travels are 1300kr. Open Mon–Sat lunch and dinner.

Noma $$$$ *Strandgade 93, DK-1401 Copenhagen K; tel: 32 96 32 97; www.noma.dk.* Noma has two Michelin stars, and was named the world's best restaurant in 2010, 2011 and 2012 by *Restaurant* magazine. As you may imagine, it's tough to get a table – reservations are taken two months in advance and are snapped up instantly. Those lucky enough to get in can experience the 20-course food-as-theatre tasting menu (1500kr) based on Nordic delicacies: horse mussels, deep-sea crabs and langoustines, truffles and musk ox, alongside the best beef, lamb and elderberries and the purest water from Greenland. Open Tue–Sat lunch and dinner.

Spiseloppen $$ *Badsmandsstræde 43, Christiania, Copenhagen K; tel: 32 57 95 58; http://spiseloppen.dk.* This super-cosy restaurant, run as a collective, has a daily changing menu, influenced by styles and flavours from all over the world. It's above the Loppen club – don't be put off by the scary-looking stairs. Open Tue–Sun from 5pm.

Restaurant Viva $$ *Langebrogade Kaj 570, DK-1411 Copenhagen K; tel: 27 25 05 05; www.restaurantviva.dk.* Based inside a ship moored in the harbour by Langebro, this seafood restaurant seats 70 inside and another 50 on the sun deck in the summer. It offers plenty of shellfish specialities, stylish decor and the sensation of being on board a ship when a passing speedboat raises waves. Open daily lunch and dinner; closed mid–end July.

NØRREBRO

Kiin Kiin $$$$ *Guldbergsgade 21, DK-2200 Copenhagen N; tel: 35 35 75 55; www.kiin.dk.* 'Eat Eat' in Thai, this restaurant on trendy Sankt Hans Square in Nørrebro has earned the highest reviews in the Danish media and is the only Thai restaurant in the world with a Michelin star. The set tasting menu is made up of creative dishes exploding with flavour. Open Mon–Sat dinner.

Radio $–$$ *Julius Thomsens Gade 12, DK-1632 Copenhagen V; tel: 25 10 27 33; http://restaurantradio.dk.* Set up in 2011 by Noma founder Claus Meyer, Radio has won endless plaudits from the Danish media for its fabulous food. Prices are kept reasonable by packing in the tables, and turning over several sittings every night. On the border of Frederiksberg and Nørrebro, near the Forum Metro station. Open Tue–Sat from 5.30pm, also lunch Fri–Sat.

Spiseri $–$$ *Griffenfeldsgade 28, DK-2200 Copenhagen N; tel: 42 36 02 22; http://spiseri.dk.* Spiseri is one of several good-value restaurants in this up-and-coming area. It serves tasty Italian food in a cosy interior, decorated with a hotpotch of chairs and china. Open Wed–Sat 5.30pm–midnight.

A–Z TRAVEL TIPS

A Summary of Practical Information

A Accommodation ...118
   Airport 118
B Bicycle Rental 119
   Budgeting for
      Your Trip 119
C Car Hire 119
   Climate 120
   Clothing...........120
   Crime and Safety...120
D Disabled Travellers. .120
   Driving............121
E Electricity..........121
   Embassies and
      Consulates 121
   Emergencies.......122
G Gay and Lesbian
      Travellers........122
   Getting There......122
   Guides and Tours...123
H Health and
      Medical Care 124

L Language 125
   Lost Property......126
M Media.............126
   Money 127
O Opening Times.....127
P Police 128
   Post Offices 128
   Public Holidays.....128
T Telephones 129
   Time Zones 129
   Tipping............129
   Toilets.............130
   Tourist
      Information......130
   Transport 130
V Visas and Entry
      Requirements ...132
W Websites and
      Internet Access ..132
Y Youth Hostels......132

A

ACCOMMODATION (See also Youth Hostels and see page 133 for Recommended Hotels)

Hotels belonging to the Association of the Hotel, Restaurant and Tourism Industry in Denmark (HORESTA) are classified on a scale of one to five stars, based on facilities offered. The Copenhagen Visitor Centre (see page 130) can book accommodation for a 100kr fee.

Rooms in private homes are listed by Dansk Bed & Breakfast (www.bedandbreakfast.dk); but note that, in spite of the name, breakfast is rarely included! Visitors on longer breaks might consider an apartment: the Hay 4 You (Vimmelskaftet 49, 1st floor; tel: 26 28 08 25; www.hay4you.com) agency offers a variety of cosy local choices.

> How much is a room for one person/two people? **Hvad koster et enkeltværelse/dobbeltværelse?**
> Is breakfast included? **Er der morgenmad?**

AIRPORT

Copenhagen Airport, Kastrup (CPH; www.cph.dk), around 10km (6 miles) southeast of the city centre, is the main northern European hub.

There are trains every 10 minutes to Hovedbanegård, Copenhagen's Central Station; and the Metro runs roughly every four minutes into the city centre. Both leave from Terminal 3 (where all passengers go for baggage reclaim and customs). They take about 14 minutes and cost 36kr. Buses run less frequently and they take more time.

Taxis take 20–30 minutes; expect to pay 250–350kr, depending on the time of day.

B

BICYCLE RENTAL

Copenhagen's famous free City-Bike scheme will not be running in 2013 due to a lack of funding. However, many hotels offer guests free bicycles. You can also rent a decent bike from a bike shop, such as Københavns Cyklebørs (tel: 33 14 07 17; www.cykelboersen. dk) or Pedal Atleten (tel: 33 11 28 63; http://pedalatleten.dk). This costs about 75–85kr per day for a three-speeder. Bikes can be put on S-tog trains except during rush hours. Look for carriages with a cycle symbol.

BUDGETING FOR YOUR TRIP

Money-saving tips. Many museums (including the National Museum) are free, or have one day a week where admission is free. A Copenhagen Card (see page 130) can be good value, depending on which sights you see and how much public transport you use. To save money on a bus tour, hop on bus 11, which runs a circular route around the whole city for the price of a normal bus ticket. Many restaurants offer a good-value *dagens ret* (daily special).

C

CAR HIRE (see also Driving)

Having a car in Copenhagen is a hindrance rather than a help. The public-transport system is superb, and car rental, fuel and parking costs are quite high.

If you decide to hire a car once you are in Copenhagen, you could contact Avis, tel: 70 24 77 07, www.avis.dk; Europcar, tel: 70 11 33 55, www.europcar.dk; Hertz, tel: 33 17 90 20, www.hertzdk.dk; or Budget, tel: 33 55 05 00, www.budget.dk. You will need a valid national (or international) driving licence and must be at least 20 years of age (25 for some companies). Most agencies require payment by credit card.

CLIMATE

Denmark's relatively temperate climate is due to its situation and the sea currents, but frequent switches in the wind also bring changeable weather. Spring may come late, but summer is often sunny and autumn mild. You can check the weather forecast at www.dmi.dk. Average monthly temperatures in Copenhagen are:

	J	F	M	A	M	J	J	A	S	O	N	D
°C	1	0	2	6	11	16	17	16	13	9	5	2
°F	33	32	35	42	52	60	63	61	56	48	40	36

CLOTHING

Danes have a relaxed dress code, with the smart-casual look suitable for nearly every occasion.

Summer nights are long and light but often chilly; bring a cardigan and a light raincoat in addition to ordinary summer clothes. On the beach, you can be as undressed as you like. Pack plenty of warm clothes (plus a raincoat) for winter. In all seasons, comfortable walking shoes are highly recommended for your excursions on foot around town.

CRIME AND SAFETY (See also Emergencies and Police)

The Mercer Personal Safety Ranking 2011 ranks Copenhagen as one of the top-10 safest capital cities in Europe. Pickpocketing rises during the summer months: take normal precautions, particularly in crowded areas.

D

DISABLED TRAVELLERS

The Danes are generally very thoughtful about the needs of travellers with disabilities. God Adgang (http://godadgang.dk) is an Accessibility Label Scheme that keeps a searchable database of hotels, restaurants, shops, performance venues and tourist attractions that are accessible to people with disabilities.

Trains are equipped with lifts and ramps, and have disabled toilets. All Metro stations have lifts and most buses have collapsible ramps for the middle doors and a call button.

DRIVING

If you take your car into Denmark from the UK then you will need a valid driver's licence, car registration papers, a Green Card (an extension of your regular insurance policy, valid for travel abroad), a red warning triangle in case of breakdown and a national identity sticker for your car. British car-owners should note that left-dipping headlights are illegal. Headlights are compulsory at all hours. Drive on the right, pass on the left.

Drinking and driving. The law is stringent: if you are discovered to have a blood-alcohol content of more than 0.05 percent while driving, you face severe penalties.

E

ELECTRICITY

The supply for electrical appliances in Denmark is 220 volt, 50 Hz AC, and requires standard two-pin, round continental plugs. Visitors should bring their own adaptors.

EMBASSIES AND CONSULATES

The embassies, with consulate sections, are generally open Mon–Fri 8am–4pm, but there is usually a 24-hour telephone service. New Zealand does not have an embassy in Denmark.

Australia: embassy: Dampfærgevej 26, 2nd floor, DK-2100 Copenhagen Ø; tel: 70 26 36 76; www.denmark.embassy.gov.au.

Republic of Ireland: embassy: Østbanegade 21, DK-2100 Copenhagen Ø; tel: 35 47 32 00; www.embassyofireland.dk.

South Africa: embassy: Gammel Vartov Vej 8, DK-2900 Hellerup; tel: 39 18 01 85; www.southafrica.dk.

UK: embassy: Kastelsvej 36–40, DK-2100 Copenhagen Ø; tel: 35 44 52 00; http://ukindenmark.fco.gov.uk.

EMERGENCIES (See also Police and Health and Medical Care)

The all-purpose emergency number is 112 and is free from public phone boxes. Ask for police, fire or ambulance. Speak distinctly (English will be understood) and state your number and location.

To speak with a doctor during the day, ask your hotel to help. After hours (4pm–8am) and weekends, call the on-call GP on 38 69 38 69. There is also a 24-hour, 365-day helpline staffed by nurses who can advise on medical questions, and tell you which emergency clinic has the shortest waiting time – tel: 1813.

Dental emergency. Tandlægevagten, Oslo Plads 14, is a walk-in centre for out-of-hours dental emergencies, open Mon–Fri 8–9.30pm, Sat–Sun and public holidays 10am–noon and 8–9.30pm. Cash payment only.

> Can I use your phone? **Må jeg låne din telefon?**
> I have lost my bag/wallet. **Jeg har mistet min taske/tegnebog.**

G

GAY AND LESBIAN TRAVELLERS

Copenhagen has a thriving gay scene, and there are bars, clubs and a few hotels where gays are openly welcome. For information, contact LGBT Denmark, Nygade 7; tel: 33 13 19 48; www.lgbt.dk.

GETTING THERE

Air travel. The following airlines are among those operating regular services to Copenhagen **from the UK (the phone numbers**

given are for calling from the UK): SAS (Scandinavian Airlines System; tel: 0871 226 7760; www.flysas.com), Norwegian Air (tel: 0208 099 7254; www.norwegian.com), British Airways (tel: 0844 493 0787; www.britishairways.com), easyJet (tel: 0843 104 5000; www.easyjet.com).

From Australia and New Zealand: Flights to Copenhagen necessitate two, sometimes three, changes, usually in the Far East and then Europe.

Rail travel. You can travel to Copenhagen by train from London Liverpool Street to Harwich, then by DFDS Seaways to Esbjerg and onwards by train to Copenhagen (tel: 0871 522 9955; www.dfdsseaways.co.uk). Alternatively, you can take the Eurostar from St Pancras International, London, to Copenhagen (Rail Europe; tel: 0844 848 4078; www.raileurope.co.uk), via Brussels and Cologne.

GUIDES AND TOURS

The Association of Authorised Guides offers individual and group tours (tel: 33 11 33 10; www.guides.dk; Mon 11am–3.30pm, Wed and Fri 10am–3.30pm).

Canal and harbour tours. Canal Tours Copenhagen (tel: 32 96 30 00; www.stromma.dk) and Netto Boats (tel: 32 54 41 02; www.netto-baadene.dk) run 60-minute guided canal tours mid-January to mid-December, with around two to five departures per hour. Boats run from 10am to 7pm in July and Aug, shorter hours during the rest of the year. Canal Tours Copenhagen boats depart from Nyhavn and Gammel Strand; Netto tours depart from Nyhavn and Holmens Church. Strömma also runs the 'hop-on-hop-off' boat, with a free audioguide. Kayak Tours (tel: 40 50 40 06; www.kajakole.dk) depart from Gammel Strand for 1.5 to 3-hour canal voyages in kayaks equipped with intercom.

City tours. City Sightseeing (tel: 32 66 00 00; www.stromma.dk) 'hop-on-hop-off' bus tours depart from in front of the Radisson Blu Royal Hotel at Rådhuspladsen (City Hall Square) every 30 minutes from Apr–Oct. The company also runs City & Harbour Tours, combined bus-and-boat tours which last 2.5 hours and depart from mid-May to Sept 9.30am and 2.30pm.

Cycling and running. Several companies offer guided bike tours, including a three-hour whiz round the city with Bike-Mike (tel: 26 39 56 88; www.bikecopenhagenwithmike.dk). For energetic types there are also jogging tours (try running-copenhagen.dk or www.runningtours.dk).

Trips to Sweden. An 'Øresund Rundt' ('Around the Sound') ticket (199kr) gives you 48 hours to make a Malmö-Helsingborg-Helsingør-Copenhagen round trip, using the Øresund Bridge in one direction and the ferry in the other: purchase it from Copenhagen Visitor Centre.

H

HEALTH AND MEDICAL CARE

Make sure your health insurance covers any illness or accident while travelling.

In Denmark, treatment and even hospitalisation is free for any tourist taken suddenly ill or involved in an accident. For minor treatments, doctors, dentists and pharmacists will charge on the spot. For EU members, this money will be partly refunded at the local Danish health service office on production of receipts and a European Health Insurance Card (EHIC; www.ehic.org.uk), obtainable online.

A Danish pharmacy *(apotek)* is strictly a dispensary. Pharmacies are listed in the phone book under *Apoteker*. Opening hours are generally Mon–Fri 9am–5.30pm, Sat until 1pm. An all-night service operates at Steno Apotek, Vesterbrogade 6C, tel: 33 14 82 66, near the main train station.

I need a doctor/dentist. **Jeg har brug for en læge/tandlæge.**

L

LANGUAGE

English is widely spoken and understood. Danish is almost impossible to pronounce simply by reading the words, as many syllables are swallowed rather than spoken. Thus the island of Amager becomes Am-air, with the 'g' disappearing, but in a distinctively Danish way difficult for the visitor to imitate. The letter 'd' becomes something like a 'th', but with the tongue placed behind the lower teeth, not the upper. The letter 'ø' is like the 'u' in English 'nurse', but spoken with the lips far forward. And the letter 'r' is again swallowed.

There are 29 letters in the Danish alphabet including 'æ' (as in egg), 'ø', and 'å' (as in port). They appear after the usual 26 (a point to note when looking up names in phone books and lists).

Days

Monday **mandag**	Friday **fredag**
Tuesday **tirsdag**	Saturday **lørdag**
Wednesday **onsdag**	Sunday **søndag**
Thursday **torsdag**	

Months

January **januar**	July **juli**
February **februar**	August **august**
March **marts**	September **september**
April **april**	October **oktober**
May **maj**	November **november**
June **juni**	December **december**

Numbers

0 **nul**	10 **ti**	20 **tyve**
1 **en**	11 **elleve**	30 **tredive**
2 **to**	12 **tolv**	40 **fyrre**
3 **tre**	13 **tretten**	50 **halvtreds**
4 **fire**	14 **fjorten**	60 **tres**
5 **fem**	15 **femten**	70 **halvfjerds**
6 **seks**	16 **seksten**	80 **firs**
7 **syv**	17 **sytten**	90 **halvfems**
8 **otte**	18 **atten**	100 **hundrede**
9 **ni**	19 **nitten**	1000 **tusind**

LOST PROPERTY

The general lost-property office *(hittegodskontor)* is at the police station at Slotsherrensvej 113, Vanløse (tel: 38 74 88 22; Mon, Wed, Fri 9am–2pm, Tue and Thur 9am–5.30pm). For property lost on trains, contact the S-train information office (tel: 36 14 17 01; daily 7am–11pm). For missing credit cards use the following numbers: American Express, tel: +44 1273 696 933; Diners Club, tel: +44 1252 513 500. To block Visa, MasterCard and other cards: PBS 24-hour hotline, tel: 44 89 27 50.

MEDIA

Newspapers and magazines. English-language newspapers and magazines are widely available at news-stands, shops and hotels. The free monthly English-language booklet *Copenhagen This Week* contains comprehensive visitor information. *The **Copenhagen Post,*** a weekly newspaper that prints Danish news in English, has a good listings guide.

MONEY

Currency. The unit of Danish currency is the kroner, abbreviated to kr, or, abroad, DKK (to distinguish it from the Norwegian and Swedish kroner). It is divided into 100 øre. Coin denominations are 50 øre and 1, 2, 5, 10 and 20 kroner. Banknotes: 50, 100, 200, 500 and 1,000 kroner.

Credit cards and traveller's cheques. Most institutions will accept payment by most international credit cards. Credit cards are not accepted in many pharmacies.

Tax. Danish VAT is called MOMS and is set at 25 percent. It's always included in the bill. Foreign visitors can claim a tax refund if they spend over 300kr in a single shop displaying the Global Tax-Free Shopping sign. Ask the cashier for a tax-free form, then take it to Tax Free Worldwide (www.taxfreeworldwide.com) or Global Blue (www.global-blue.com), who have desks in the airport and the large department stores, for a 20 percent refund. Alternatively, you can post your tax-free form.

Do you accept credit cards? **Godtager I kreditkort?**
Can you change a traveller's cheque for me? **Kan jeg indløse en rejsecheck?**

OPENING TIMES

Banks. Open Mon–Fri 9.30am–4pm, Thur until 6pm. In the provinces, hours fluctuate from town to town.

Museums. Often closed on Monday and generally open for shorter hours during the winter.

Shops. Hours vary from business to business, but general opening times are Mon–Thur 10am–6pm, Fri 10am–7pm, Sat 10am–4pm and Sun noon–4pm.

P

POLICE (See also Emergencies)

State and city police all form part of the national force and are dressed in dark-blue uniforms. Most policemen patrol in dark-blue-and-white or white cars with the word *politi* in large letters. Police are courteous and speak English.

The emergency number is 112. For non-emergencies, phone 114 to be connected to the nearest local police station. Main Copenhagen police station: Politigården, Polititorvet 1, tel: 33 14 14 48.

POST OFFICES

In general, post offices are open 9 or 10am–5 or 6pm during the week; some post offices are also open on Sat 9am–noon.

There are two very central post offices at Købmagergade 33 (by the Post & Tele Museum) and at Vesterbrogade 8 (near the Liberty Column) that both open Mon–Fri 10am–6pm, Sat 10am–2pm. The post office at Central Station operates longer hours: Mon–Fri 8am–9pm, Sat–Sun 10am–4pm. All post offices display a red sign with a crown, bugle and crossed arrows in yellow – and a sign saying *Kongelig Post og Telegraf*. Danish postboxes are bright red.

PUBLIC HOLIDAYS

Though Denmark's banks, offices and major shops close on public holidays, museums, cafés and tourist attractions will mostly be open. Although Christmas Eve and New Year's Eve are not official holidays, most shops, businesses and attractions close on those days too.

1 January: Nytårsdag, New Year's Day
5 June (half-day): Grundslovsdag, Constitution Day
25/26 December: Christmas
Moveable dates:
Skærtorsdag, Maundy Thursday
Langfredag, Good Friday

Anden påskedag, Easter Monday
Store Bededag, General Prayer Day (fourth Friday after Easter)
Kristi himmelfartsdag, Ascension Day
Anden pinsedag, Whit Monday

T

TELEPHONES

The country code for Denmark is 45. Local Danish numbers have eight digits, and there are no area codes.

To call Denmark from the UK: dial 00 + 45 + the personal telephone number.

To make international calls from Denmark: dial 00 + the country code + the area code (omitting the first 0 for UK numbers) + the personal telephone number.

Mobile telephones. Danish mobile phones operate on the 900/1800 Mhz GSM network – most unlocked European phones will work. US visitors will only be able to use their mobile in Denmark if it is a tri-band phone that can switch bands.

Public telephone boxes. Most take prepaid phone cards from kiosks, supermarkets and petrol stations. Some take credit cards/coins.

TIME ZONES

Denmark follows Central European Time (GMT + 1). In summer, the clock is put one hour ahead (GMT + 2). Time differences are:

New York	London	Copenhagen	Jo'burg	Sydney
7am	noon	**1pm**	1pm	9pm

TIPPING

Tipping is not obligatory in Denmark, as most hotel and restaurant staff are paid proper salaries.

TOILETS

Facilities are usually indicated by a pictograph; alternatively they are marked WC, *Toiletter, Damer/Herrer* (Ladies/Gentlemen), or just D/H. There is no charge unless you see it clearly marked otherwise.

TOURIST INFORMATION

The Copenhagen Visitor Centre, 4a Vesterbrogade, across from Central Station and just outside Tivoli (open July–Aug Mon–Sat 9am–8pm, Sun 10am–6pm; May–June Mon–Sat 9am–6pm, Sun 10am–2pm; Sept–Apr Mon–Fri 9am–4pm, Sat 9am–2pm; tel: 70 22 24 42; www.visitcopenhagen.com), offers a comprehensive array of tourist information, and assistance with booking sightseeing tours and accommodation.

Copenhagen Card. The Copenhagen Visitor Centre is also one of the many places where you can purchase the Copenhagen Card. The card lasts for 24, 72 or 120 hours and gives free or reduced admission to more than 70 popular museums and sights in the city. It also grants free travel on buses, S-trains, Metro and the harbour bus throughout the region, as well as discounts on car hire and the Scandlines Helsingør-Helsingborg ferry service between Denmark and Sweden. The 24/72/120-hour cards cost 249/479/699kr (children 10–15 years 119/239/349kr), and two children under 10 years may accompany each adult free of charge.

UK: VisitDenmark, 55 Sloane Street, London SW1X 9SY; tel: 020 7259 5959; email contact@visitdenmark.com.

TRANSPORT

An excellent integrated public-transport system covers not only Copenhagen but also its extensive metropolitan area. The area is divided into zones, with fares charged according to how many zones you pass through. The system makes travel simple: the same tickets are used on buses, S-trains, the harbour bus and the Metro. A basic ticket permits travel within two zones for one hour and costs 24kr (12kr for children aged 0–15). You must clip your ticket when you get on the bus, or on the train platform before you get on. A 24-hour all-zone ticket costs 130kr (65kr for children) and permits 24 hours of unlimited travel. Discount clip cards *(klippekort)* are available for 10 journeys. Travel between 1am and 5am costs double the daytime fare. Two under-12s can travel free with an adult who has a valid ticket.

Buses. Operated by Movia (tel: 36 13 14 15; www.moviatrafik.dk), buses run daily between 5am and 12.30am. There are additional night buses from Rådhuspladsen to the suburbs. Buses are yellow and you get on at the front and off at the back.

Harbour Bus. The blue-and-yellow boats (www.moviatrafik.dk) run six times an hour (6am–6pm) through the harbour, between the Royal Library on Christians Brygge and the Little Mermaid, with stops at Nyhavn and Holmen North.

Metro. Automated Metro trains (tel: 70 15 16 15; http://intl.m.dk) run on two lines – M1 and M2 – every 4–6 minutes in the daytime, and every 15–20 minutes through the night. The ambitious Cityringen circle extension will create two new lines and 17 new stations by 2018.

S-Train. Run by DSB S-Tog (tel: 33 14 17 01; www.dsb.dk), red S-tog local trains link Copenhagen with other towns on Sjælland.

Taxis. Taxis are recognisable by a *Taxi* or *Taxa* sign, and vacant cabs display the word *fri* **(free)**. Tipping is not necessary, but round the sum up if you are impressed by the service. The basic fare is 24kr, plus 14kr per km Mon–Fri 7am–4pm; 17.90kr Fri–Sat 11pm–7am; and 15kr per km at other times. Most drivers accept credit cards.

Trains. A comprehensive and generally punctual network, which covers the entire country, operates from Copenhagen Central Station.

How much is a ticket to...? **Hvad koster en billet to...?**
One ticket to..., please. **En billet til..., tak.**
Where does this train/bus go? **Hvor kører dette tog/denne bus hen?**

V

VISAS AND ENTRY REQUIREMENTS

Visitors from Britain and countries outside the EU need a valid passport to enter Denmark; citizens from EU countries, excluding Britain, need only an identity card. Visitors from the UK, USA, EU, Australia and New Zealand are generally entitled to stay in Denmark for up to 90 days without a visa (this period includes the total amount of time spent in Denmark, Finland, Iceland, Norway and Sweden in any six-month period).

South African citizens require a visa. See the Danish Embassy in South Africa website for further information: http://sydafrika. um.dk.

W

WEBSITES AND INTERNET ACCESS

There is comprehensive tourist information at www.visitcopenhagen.com. Catch up with the Danish news in English at *The Copenhagen Post* website http://cphpost.dk, and investigate the quirks of Danish society at http://denmark.dk. Discover Copenhagen's hottest pubs, clubs, restaurants, shops and shows on the *AOK* listings magazine website http://www.aok.dk/english.

Many cafés and hotels offer a wireless internet service. There is also free internet access in Danish libraries.

Y

YOUTH HOSTELS

There are 13 central youth hostels in the city, four of which are run by Danhostel Danmarks Vandrerhjem, Vesterbrogade 39, DK-1620 Copenhagen V; tel: 31 31 36 12; www.danhostel.dk. A dorm bed costs around 160–250kr.

Recommended Hotels

Most of Copenhagen's hotels are clustered near the city's main sights – Rådhuspladsen, Tivoli Gardens, the University Quarter and the lively shopping area along Strøget.

The following hotels are listed alphabetically, area by area. The price categories are based on the cost per night of a double room with bath or shower in the high season, including service charges and tax (but not breakfast, which is usually an extra, costing 100kr to 180kr). However, rates are often based on demand and can vary hugely: even at expensive hotels, they can be as much as 50 percent lower at other times of the year. Look out for deals or ring to ask if any are available. Booking on the internet (and also via comparison sites) can also be cheaper.

It is always advisable to reserve ahead of your stay. The city is at its busiest in the summer months (June–August), but conferences ensure that hotels are kept busy throughout the year.

Check out the excellent overview on www.visitcopenhagen.dk, where you can also make bookings.

$$$$	over 2,000kr
$$$	1,500–2,000kr
$$	1,000–1,500kr
$	under 1,000kr

AROUND RÅDHUSPLADSEN AND VESTERBRO

Hotel Alexandra $$$ *H.C. Andersens Boulevard 8, DK-1553 Copenhagen V; tel: 33 74 44 44; www.hotelalexandra.dk.* This lovely old hotel, in a building originating from the 1880s, is almost next door to Rådhuspladsen. It's stylishly decorated, with light, airy rooms and excellent facilities – the 13 'Danish Design' rooms, each furnished in tribute to a particular designer, are worth the extra cost. 61 rooms.

Andersen Hotel $$$–$$$ *Helgolandsgade 128, DK-1653 Copenhagen V; tel: 33 31 46 10; www.andersen-hotel.dk.* Since its opening in

2012, this cheerful little boutique hotel has been wowing the crowds. Rooms are on the cosy side: if you like your space, plump for a deluxe or superior. Some internet rates include a fabulous breakfast. The hotel is handy for the stylish restaurants in the old Meatpacking District (Kødbyen). 72 rooms.

Carlton Hotel Guldsmeden $ *Vesterbrogade 66, DK-1620 Copenhagen V; tel: 33 22 15 00; www.hotelguldsmeden.dk.* A great little three-star hotel, decorated in cosy colonial style and located in the lively Vesterbro neighbourhood. Equally charming is sister-hotel Bertrams Hotel Guldsmeden ($$; Vesterbrogade 107; tel: 33 25 04 05), with a relaxing courtyard garden, a few blocks further down Vesterbrogade. Both provide tasty organic breakfasts with bread from a nearby gourmet bakery. Carlton 64 rooms; Bertrams 47 rooms.

Clarion Collection Hotel Mayfair $$–$$$ *Helgolandsgade 3, DK-1653 Copenhagen V; tel: 70 12 17 00; www.choicehotels.dk.* This little gem offers a friendly atmosphere, cosy rooms and a very high standard of personal service. A continental breakfast, hot drinks, afternoon cakes and a light evening buffet are included in the price – very helpful to those on a budget. 106 rooms.

Copenhagen Marriott Hotel $$$$ *Kalvebod Brygge 5, DK-1560 Copenhagen V; tel: 88 33 99 00; www.marriott.com/cphdk.* A luxury glass and concrete block offers all that one expects from Marriott hotels, including some of the biggest rooms in Copenhagen. Waterside rooms overlook the inner harbour. 401 rooms.

Copenhagen Plaza $$$$ *Bernstorffsgade 4, DK-1577 Copenhagen V; tel: 33 14 92 62; www.profilhotels.dk.* Commissioned by Frederik VIII in 1913, this hotel has old-fashioned style and a historic elevator with a mind of its own! Rooms are decently-sized – reserve one on a higher floor for impressive city views. The wood-panelled, leather-seated Library Bar has its own jazz pianist and professional cocktail-maker. 93 rooms.

Copenhagen Star Hotel $$$ *Colbjørnsensgade 13, DK-1652 Copenhagen V; tel: 33 22 11 00; www.copenhagenstar.dk.* Situated in the cluster of streets on the other side of Central Station from Tivoli, with well-appointed rooms. A good breakfast buffet is included in the rates. 134 rooms.

Danhostel Copenhagen Downtown $ *Vandkunsten 5, DK-1467 Copenhagen K; tel: 70 23 21 10;* http://copenhagendowntown.com. The pick of the central hostels, this friendly, funky place has excellent facilities. The lively bar is a great place to meet fellow travellers, or you can borrow iPads and laptops from reception to contact the folk back home.

Hotel Danmark $$ *Vester Voldgade 89, DK-1552 Copenhagen V; tel: 33 11 48 06;* www.hotel-danmark.dk. Adjacent to Rådhuspladsen and close to Strøget, this modern bright building has rooms tastefully furnished in subdued Scandinavian style. 88 rooms.

First Hotel Kong Frederik $$$ *Vester Voldgade 25, DK-1552 Copenhagen V; tel: 33 12 59 02;* www.firsthotels.com. Close to Rådhuspladsen and Tivoli. A 2010 renovation retained the classic 'English' atmosphere in public areas, while the bedrooms are modern Scandinavian. Some overlook the internal atrium, while others spy on the busy street. 110 rooms.

First Hotel Vesterbro $–$$$ *Vesterbrogade 23–29, DK-1620 Copenhagen V; tel: 33 78 80 00;* www.firsthotels.dk/vesterbro. This modern hotel has a great location in trendy Vesterbro. Its decent-sized rooms are decorated with warm cherry-wood furniture; the quieter ones look down onto the internal atrium where breakfast is served. Just a five-minute walk from Rådhuspladsen. 403 rooms.

Grand Hotel $$–$$$ *Vesterbrogade 9A, DK-1620 Copenhagen V; tel: 33 27 69 00;* www.grandhotel.dk. An attractive facade, dating from 1890, fronts a carefully modernised and tastefully decorated hotel. The Ristorante Frascati serves great Italian food at night. 161 rooms.

Imperial Hotel $$$ *Vester Farimagsgade 9, DK-1606 Copenhagen V; tel: 33 12 80 00;* www.imperialhotel.dk. In a good location next to Vesterport Station, a few minutes' walk from Rådhuspladsen and

Tivoli Gardens. Modern, well-appointed, with elegant rooms, fine restaurants and on-site parking. 163 rooms.

Nimb $$$$ *Tivoli, Bernstorffsgade 5, DK-1630 Copenhagen V; tel: 88 70 00 00*; www.tivoli.dk. A romantic's dream, Nimb is in a Moorish-style palace, beautifully illuminated at night, inside Tivoli gardens. Its 14 fabulous boutique rooms contain a deeply satisfying blend of modern and antique furniture, and sleek bathrooms come with bathtubs and double sinks. If you're here in winter, working fire-places add to the romance. Entry to Tivoli is included in the price. 14 rooms.

Radisson Blu Royal Hotel $$$–$$$$ *Hammerichsgade 1, DK-1611 Copenhagen V; tel: 33 42 60 00*; www.radissonblu.com. Dating from 1960, this iconic 20-storey hotel (designed, down to the cutlery and door knobs, by architect Arne Jacobsen) offers a panoramic view of Tivoli Gardens and the city. Rooms are in modern Danish style, al-though Room 606 retains its original 1960s decor. There's a rooftop restaurant, sauna and private parking. 260 rooms.

Scandic Palace Hotel $$$$ *Rådhuspladsen 57, DK-1550 Copenha-gen V; tel: 33 14 40 50*; www.scandichotels.dk. An imposing historical landmark on Rådhuspladsen, the Palace has been carefully renovat-ed and modernised in recent years to the highest standards. Superior rooms are worth paying extra for: ask for one on a higher floor with a balcony for good city views. 169 rooms.

Scandic Webers $$–$$$ *Vesterbrogade 11B, DK-1620 Copenhagen V; tel: 33 31 44 32*; www.scandichotels.dk. Scandic hotels offer business and leisure travellers reliably comfortable rooms and good facilities, and the Webers conforms to type. It has a trendy bar and peaceful courtyard, and guests have free access to the Scandic Copenhagen's gym/sauna. 152 rooms.

The Square $$$–$$$$ *Rådhuspladsen 14, DK-1550 Copenhagen V; tel: 33 38 12 00*; www.thesquare.dk. Right on Rådhuspladsen, this sleek design hotel offers several grades of rooms, smiling staff and a rooftop breakfast room with fine views. 192 rooms (46 singles).

Wakeup Copenhagen $ *Carsten Niebuhrs Gade 11, DK-1577 Copenhagen V; tel: 44 80 00 00; www.wakeupcopenhagen.com*. Designed by Kim Utzon, this budget hotel has clean, compact rooms with flatscreen TVs and free Wi-fi. Prices rise as you go higher up the building – the 'Wakeup Heaven' rooms on the top floor have the best views. The hotel represents good value in an expensive city.

Zleep Hotel Astoria $ *Banegårdspladsen 4, DK-1570 Copenhagen V; tel: 70 23 56 35; www.zleephotels.com*. Dating from 1936, this budget hotel's bizarre facade is an excellent architectural example of Cubist style. It's right next to the main train station – light sleepers may struggle in rooms on the track side. 94 rooms.

AROUND KONGENS NYTORV

Hotel d'Angleterre $$$$ *Kongens Nytorv 34, DK-1050 Copenhagen K; tel: 33 12 00 95; www.dangleterre.dk*. Established more than 250 years ago, this five-star 'fairy-tale' hotel has traditionally provided a refuge for the rich and famous. It has been closed for several years, undergoing a total overhaul, and was due to reopen in May 2013.

Hotel Opera $$$ *Tordenskjoldsgade 15, DK-1055 Copenhagen K; tel: 33 47 83 00; www.hotelopera.dk*. Dating from 1869, this charming three-star hotel is close to the Royal Theatre. Some of its 'English-inspired' rooms are on the small side – request a larger one if you like more space. 91 rooms.

UNIVERSITY QUARTER AND PARKS

Ascot Hotel $$$ *Studiestræde 61, DK-1554 Copenhagen V; tel: 33 12 60 00; www.ascot-hotel.dk*. In a distinguished old bathhouse building in the Latin Quarter, this hotel is decorated with a mixture of antiques and modern furniture – some rooms are fresher than others. Mini-apartments are also available. 190 rooms.

Hotel Christian IV $$–$$$ *Dronningens Tværgade 45, DK-1302 Copenhagen K; tel: 33 32 10 44; www.hotelchristianiv.dk*. A small, highly pleasing hotel right by the lovely King's Garden. Rooms are neat and bright, and fitted with modern Danish furniture, and rates include a good breakfast spread. Quiet neighbourhood. 42 rooms.

First Hotel Skt Petri $$$–$$$$ *Krystalgade 22, DK-1172 Copenhagen K; tel: 33 45 91 00; www.firsthotels.com.* This award-winning five-star design hotel shows great attention to detail, right down to the electronica music that its staff commission and pipe into the lifts. In summer, there is also an attractive outdoor area for drinks and dinner. 27 suites, 268 rooms.

Hotel Fox $$–$$$ *Jarmers Plads 3, DK-1551 Copenhagen V; tel: 33 13 30 00; www.hotelfox.dk.* A truly unique hotel: each room is designed differently by one of 21 young international artists. Some rooms are cool, some very strange: they are due to be refreshed and updated soon, but until then, the prices have been reduced. Located in the Latin Quarter close to cult hang-outs. 61 rooms.

Hotel Kong Arthur $$$$ *Nørre Søgade 11, DK-1370 Copenhagen V; tel: 33 11 12 12; www.kongarthur.dk.* Established in 1882, and situated beside Peblinge Lake, this appealing hotel has retained much of its original charm. A popular choice with both Danish and foreign visitors, it has a friendly and thoroughly Danish atmosphere. 155 rooms.

NYHAVN AND BEYOND

71 Nyhavn Hotel $$$–$$$$ *Nyhavn 71, DK-1051 Copenhagen K; tel: 33 43 62 00; www.71nyhavnhotel.com.* Delightfully located at the foot of Nyhavn in two well-renovated and carefully restored spice warehouses, this modern hotel has rather small rooms, a rustic atmosphere and great views over the harbour. 150 rooms.

Adina Apartment Hotel Copenhagen $$$$ *Amerikaplads 7, DK-2100 Copenhagen Ø; tel: 39 69 10 00; www.adina.eu.* These fabulous four-star hotel apartments are equipped with kitchenettes, a washer/drier, etc, and guests have access to a small gym, swimming pool and jacuzzi. Just north of the Little Mermaid and handy for the cruise-ship port. 126 rooms.

Copenhagen Admiral Hotel $$$–$$$$ *Toldbodgade 24–28, DK-1253 Copenhagen K; tel: 33 74 14 14;* www.admiralhotel.dk. Standing beside the harbour, the hotel was formerly a granary constructed in 1787. Comfortably converted, it has retained the 200-year-old Pomeranian pine wooden beams in the rooms. Features its own well-regarded brasserie restaurant and a sauna. 366 rooms.

Copenhagen Strand $$$ *Havnegade 37, DK-1058 Copenhagen K; tel: 33 48 99 00;* www.copenhagenstrand.dk. This cosy hotel, with quaint maritime touches, is in a converted warehouse dating from 1869, on a side street just off Nyhavn. 174 rooms.

Phoenix Copenhagen $$$ *Bredgade 37, DK-1260 Copenhagen K; tel: 33 95 95 00;* www.phoenixcopenhagen.dk. An elegant hotel close to the Royal Palace and Kongens Nytorv. All rooms and suites are air-conditioned and furnished in the French Louis XVI style. 213 rooms.

Scandic Front Hotel $$$$ *Sankt Annæ Plads 21, DK-1250 Copenhagen K; tel: 33 13 34 00;* www.scandichotels.com. This modern boutique hotel is on the harbour front close to Nyhavn. The rooms are sleek and well-equipped – the lovely split-level suites have face-on views of the Opera House. 132 rooms.

OUTLYING AREAS

Hilton Copenhagen Airport $$$–$$$$ *Ellehammersvej 20, DK-2770 Copenhagen; tel: 32 50 15 01;* www.hilton.dk. This hotel offers Copenhagen's largest rooms, five-star luxury and a lobby filled with famous Arne Jacobsen chairs usually holding celebrities. You can't get closer to the airport – it's just two minutes' walk to Terminal 3. 382 rooms.

Radisson Blu Scandinavia Hotel $$–$$$ *Amager Boulevard 70, DK-2300 Copenhagen S; tel: 33 96 50 00;* www.radissonblu.com/scandinaviahotel-copenhagen. A 25-storey building that dominates the skyline 1km (half a mile) from Tivoli Gardens across the water on Amager. Rooms are furnished in standard, Scandinavian or Oriental decor, and most have fine views. Convenient for the airport. 542 rooms.

INDEX

Amagermuseet 70
Amaliehavn Gardens 55
Amalienborg Palace 56
Amalienborg Palace
    Museum 57
Amber Museum 35
Arken 73
Assistens Cemetery 69

Bishop Absalon, statue
    of 37
Børsen 39
Botanisk Have 52
Bull-and-Dragon Fountain
    27

Caritas Fountain 32
Carlsberg Brewery 31
Changing of the Guard
    57
Charlottenborg Slot 35
Christiania 66
Christiansborg 39
Christianshavn 63
Christians Kirke 64
Christian VII's Palace 57
Churchill Park 58
City Hall Tower 27

Danmarks National-
    historiske Museum 79
Dansk Arkitektur Center
    64
Dansk Design Center 46
Dansk Jødisk Museum
    45
David Collection 51
Designmuseum Danmark
    61
Det Kongelige Bibliotek
    (Royal Library) 44

Domkirke (Cathedral) 47
Dragør 71

Fiskerkone, statue of 37
Folketing 41
Frederiksberg Have 67
Frederiksborg Slot 78
Frihedsmuseet (Museum
    of the Danish
    Resistance Movement
    1940–45) 58
Frilandsmuseet (Open-Air
    Folk Museum) 71

Gammelstrand 37
Gammeltorv 32
Gefion Fountain 58
Glass Museum 68
Gråbrødretorv 49
Grundtvigs Kirke 69

Helligåndskirken 33
Helsingør 75
    Carmelite Kloster 77
    Kronborg Slot 75
    M/S Maritime
        Museum of
        Denmark 77
    Skt Mariæ Kirke 77
Hillerød 78
Hirschsprungske Samling,
    Den 52
Højbro Plads 37
Holmens Kirke 36
Hotel D'Angleterre 35

Jens Olsen's World
    Clock 27

Kanneworffs Hus 35
Kastellet 60

Kødbyen 30
Kongelige Repræsen-
    tationslokaler (Royal
    Reception Chambers)
    40
Kongelige Stalde og
    Kareter (Royal Stables)
    41
Kongelige Teater, Det 34
Kongens Have 51
Kongens Nytorv 34
Kunsthal Charlottenborg
    35

Lille Havfrue, Den (Little
    Mermaid) 59
Louisiana Museum of
    Modern Art 74
Lur Players statue 27
Lyngby 72

Magasin du Nord 35
Marmorbroen 40
Marmorkirken 62
Medicinsk Museion 62
Musikmuseet 68

Nationalmuseet 45
Natural History Museum
    of Denmark 52
Nikolaj Kunsthal 36
Nyboder 60
Nyboders Mindestuer
    60
Ny Carlsberg Glyptotek
    46
Nyhavn 53
Nytorv 32

Opera House 66
Ørsteds Parken 53

Post & Tele Museum 50

Rådhus (City Hall) 26
Rådhuspladsen 25
Rosenborg Slot 51
Roskilde 80
    Domkirke 80
    Vikingeskibsmuseet 83
Royal Copenhagen 33
Royal Danish Playhouse
    55
Ruinerne af Absalons
    Borg 41

Rundetaarn (Round
    Tower) 49

Skt Hans Torv 68
Skt Nicolai Kirke 36
St Alban's Church 58
Statens Museum for Kunst
    (National Gallery of
    Denmark) 52
Strøget 31

Teatermuseet 42
Thorvaldsens Museum 42

Thotts Palae 35
Tivoli Gardens 28
Tøjhusmuseet (Arsenal
    Museum) 43
Trinitatis Kirke 49

Vandkunsten 38
Vor Frelsers Kirke 64
Vor Frue Kirke 48

Zoologisk Have (Zoo)
    67

Berlitz pocket guide

Copenhagen

Seventh Edition 2013
Reprinted 2015

Written by Norman Renouf
Updated by Fran Parnell
Edited by Tom Stainer
Art Editor: Shahid Mahmood
Series Editor: Tom Stainer
Production: Tynan Dean and Rebeka Ellam

Photography credits: All pictures by APA/
Rudy Hemmingsen except:
Corbis. 2/3M David Hall 4/5M, 104; Alamy 96;
akg19, 20; Krause & Johansen 88;

Cover picture: APA/Rudy Hemmingsen

No part of this book may be reproduced,
stored in a retrieval system or transmitted
in any form or means electronic,
mechanical, photocopying, recording
or otherwise, without prior written
permission from Berlitz Publishing. Brief
text quotations with use of photographs are
exempted for book review purposes only.

All Rights Reserved
© 2013 Apa Publications (UK) Limited
Printed in China by CTPS
Berlitz Trademark Reg. U.S. Patent Office
and other countries. Marca Registrada.
Used under licence from the Berlitz
Investment Corporation

Every effort has been made to provide
accurate information in this publication,
but changes are inevitable. The publisher
cannot be responsible for any resulting
loss, inconvenience or injury.

Contact us

At Berlitz we strive to keep our guides as
accurate and up to date as possible, but if you
find anything that has changed, or if you have
any suggestions on ways to improve this guide,
then we would be delighted to hear from you.

Berlitz Publishing, PO Box 7910,
London SE1 1WE, England.
email: berlitz@apaguide.co.uk
www.insightguides.com/berlitz

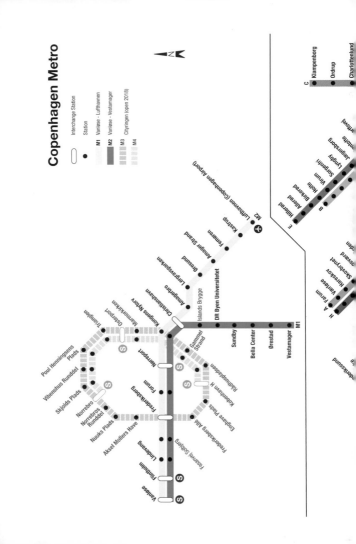

Copenhagen Metro

Interchange Station
Station
M1 Vanløse - Lufthavnen
M2 Vanløse - Vestamager
M3 Cityringen (open 2018)
M4

N

Klampenborg
Ordrup
Charlottenlund
C

Hillerød
Allerød
Birkerød
Holte
Virum
Sorgenfri
Lyngby
Jægersborg
rsborg
hotte
nsel

Skovbrynet
Værløse
Farum
A
H

dersund

Lufthavnen (Copenhagen Airport)
M2
Kastrup
Femøren
Amager Strand
Øresund
Lergravsparken
Amagerbro
Islands Brygge
DR Byen Universitetet
Sundby
Bella Center
Ørestad
Vestamager
M1

Christianshavn
Kongens Nytorv
Gammel
Strand
Rådhuspladsen
København H
Forum
Enghave Plads
Frederiksberg Allé
Fasanvej (Solbjerg)

Flintholm
Østerport
Marmorkirken
Nørreport
Frederiksberg
Poul Henningsens
Plads
Vibenshus Runddel
Skjolds Plads
Nørrebro
Nørrebros
Runddel
Nuuks Plads
Aksel Møllers Have
Lindevang
Fuglebakken
Vanløse